Only in

LAMAR
MISSOURI

Only in

LAMAR MISSOURI

Harry Truman, Wyatt Earp and Legendary Locals

Randy Turner

THE
History
PRESS

Published by The History Press
Charleston, SC
www.historypress.com

Front cover, clockwise from top left: A crowd greeted Senator Harry S. Truman as he returned to Lamar to give his vice-presidential nomination acceptance speech on August 31, 1944. Truman is shown with Texas senator Tom Connally. Photo courtesy of Truman Library and Museum; photo by Terry Redman; Naval History and Heritage Command; *Lamar Democrat*; Lamar High School cheerleaders and band march in a parade prior to the dedication of President Harry S. Truman's birthplace on April 19, 1959. Photo courtesy of Truman Library and Museum; Naval History and Heritage Command, National Archives.
Back cover: the 2013 state champion Lamar High School football team celebrates. Photo by Terry Redman; *inset*: provided by Marshall Bulle.

First published 2022

Manufactured in the United States

ISBN 9781467151412

Library of Congress Control Number: 2021952411

Notice: The information in this book is true and complete to the best of our knowledge. It is offered without guarantee on the part of the author or The History Press. The author and The History Press disclaim all liability in connection with the use of this book.

CONTENTS

Contents

PREFACE

ore than forty years have passed since I first arrived in Lamar as sports editor of the *Lamar Democrat*, the smallest daily newspaper in Missouri. Though I spent only eight months in the city at that point, when I returned to the newspaper as its managing editor in 1982, I began to better appreciate the city's rich history.

When I made my rounds at the Barton County Courthouse, I passed the monument that had been placed where candidate and Lamar native son Harry S. Truman gave his vice-presidential nomination acceptance speech in 1944.

I worked in the same building where Arthur Aull and Madeleine Aull Van Hafften served as *Lamar Democrat* editors.

I had the privilege of receiving, editing and publishing local history columns written by Wyatt Earp's cousin Reba Earp Young.

I lived in an apartment owned by Tom O'Sullivan's O'Sullivan Properties and had the pleasure of writing about members of his family.

Among the other people I interviewed during my years at the *Democrat* were some of those who were still in the process of making history and creating local legends. I was fortunate enough to interview Gerald Gilkey, the longest-serving mayor in Missouri history; banker and war hero Richard Chancellor; and a Lamar High School football and basketball star named Scott Bailey, who returned to his alma mater and guided it to a record seven straight state football championships from 2011 to 2017.

It is difficult to find a city the size of Lamar, Missouri, that has such a rich history, including not only people who made their marks locally but also those whose fame stretched far beyond the Lamar city limits.

For a city with a population of slightly more than four thousand, being known as the place where the legends of Harry Truman and Wyatt Earp began would certainly be enough of a claim for the history books. But for Lamar, it is only the beginning.

At the same time that President Truman, a Lamar native, was commander in chief, Admiral Freeland Daubin, a Lamar High School graduate, was commander of submarines for the Atlantic Fleet, and another Lamar High School graduate, Admiral Charles Lockwood, was commander of submarines for the Pacific Fleet.

Yet a third LHS graduate, Admiral Thomas Selby Combs, was chief of staff for naval aircraft in the South Pacific. The first director of the U.S. Women's Coast Guard Auxiliary was Dorothy Stratton, who did not graduate from Lamar High School but who lived in Lamar for three years and attended the high school her freshman year.

Many people with a connection to Lamar made their mark on our nation's history, but sometimes that history was being made in Lamar.

On two occasions, events that occurred in Lamar were described on page one of the *New York Times*. The September 1, 1944 *Times* featured coverage of the speech Truman made when he accepted the Democratic Party's vice-presidential nomination.

A quarter of a century earlier, the May 29, 1919 *Times* featured the much darker story of a mob of Lamar residents, allegedly including some leading citizens, that broke into the judge's chambers in the Barton County Courthouse, overwhelmed law enforcement, took the man who had just been sentenced to life in prison for murdering the sheriff and his son and hanged the man—who had the unfortunate name of Jay Lynch—from a tree in the courthouse yard.

Lamar, Missouri, was the home of legendary newspaper editor Arthur Aull, whose no-holds-barred brand of journalism brought him subscribers from across the nation, including actor-comedian W.C. Fields.

The city became the home to two large manufacturing facilities, Lawn-Boy and O'Sullivan Industries. After O'Sullivan closed its doors, putting 1,200 people out of work, community spirit was lifted by the accomplishments of a group of young men known as "The Brotherhood," the Lamar High School football teams that won seven straight state championships, a Missouri record, and that at one point had the nation's longest winning streak, at fifty-seven games.

Researching and writing this book has been a rewarding experience. It has enabled me to relive my younger days living and working in the Lamar community and allowed me to share some of the stories that make Lamar, Missouri, not only a community where legends began but also one where legends thrive.

ACKNOWLEDGEMENTS

*T*hose who accept the challenge of writing history owe a great debt to the people who paved the way with their own research and writing. I was fortunate enough to have the help of many good friends during the preparation of this book, including some who are no longer with us.

I had the good fortune to work with historian (and Wyatt Earp's cousin) Reba Earp Young, who wrote a history column for the *Lamar Democrat* when I served as the newspaper's editor from 1982 to 1990.

During my time as editor and reporter at the *Carthage Press* in the '90s, I had the privilege of working with historian Marvin Van Gilder, author of *The Story of Barton County*.

Sadly, Reba Young and Marvin Van Gilder are no longer with us, but their research and dedication to Lamar and Barton County history remain to provide guidance for those who choose to follow in their footsteps.

Chad Stebbins, author of the 1998 Arthur Aull biography *All the News Is Fit to Print*, was kind enough to share his research. In the past two years, as I have researched the information in this book, I have benefited from the help and guidance of the Barton County Historical Society, its director Pauletta Orahood and researcher and historical columnist Joe Davis.

Many others helped make this book possible, including people who graciously offered their time for interviews, helped me collect photos and kept me headed in the right direction.

I apologize if I have omitted any names. Among those who made this book possible are the following: Scott Bailey, Barton County Chamber of Commerce, Beth Bazal, Jared Beshore, Michelle Brooks, Marshall Bulle, Carthage Public Library, Louise Caruthers, Frances Cato, Eric Chancellor, Erin Chancellor, Ione Chancellor, Traci Cox, Joe Davis, Astra Ferris, Nell Finley, Courtney Gardner, John Gilkey, Katie Gilkey, Steve Gilkey, John Hacker, Kent Harris, Zach Harris, Harry S. Truman Presidential Library and Museum, Joplin Public Library, *Lamar Democrat*, Melody Metzger, Chris Morrow, Hannah Oeltjen, Pauletta Orahood, Dorothy Parks, Jill Purinton, Terry Redman, Chad Stebbins, Carolyn Taffner, Betty Thieman, Truman Birthplace, Chris Van Gilder, Holly Willhite, Larry Wood, Kari Worsley and Julie Yokley.

1
WYATT EARP

*L*amar, Missouri, advertises itself as the city "Where Legends Begin." Its two best-known legends, Harry S. Truman and Wyatt Earp, arrived in years shortly after the city's creation.

The city's founders, George Ward and Joseph Parry, settled in the area that is now Lamar in 1852. At the time, it was a wilderness area and part of Jasper County.

Ward established the city, naming it after college classmate Mirabeau Lamar, the first military governor of Texas, and successfully petitioned the legislature to establish a separate county, which was named Barton after David Barton, the first U.S. senator from Missouri.

The city's early years were difficult. During the Civil War, Confederate guerrilla leader William Quantrill raided the city on November 5, 1862, burning approximately one-third of the houses.

In 1863, Confederate sympathizers burned the Barton County Courthouse and stole county records, most of which were never recovered.

Quantrill returned on May 20, 1864, to Lamar, where Union troops had been stationed, but most had moved to Neosho after a rumor that Quantrill was planning a raid in that community.

Though Quantrill's raid was largely unsuccessful—he ended up losing thirty men—Lamar was attacked again eight days later by guerrillas led by Captains William Marchbanks and Henry Taylor, who laid siege to the city, burning all but one home.

In 1868, Nicholas Porter Earp and his family moved to Lamar, where he subsequently became justice of the peace. Shortly after his arrival, the Barton County Court incorporated Lamar and appointed Earp's son Wyatt, who had arrived in the city a few months earlier, as constable on March 3, 1870.

Wyatt Berry Stapp Earp, twenty-one, was the fourth child of Nicholas Earp and Virginia Cooksey Earp. He was named for Captain Wyatt Berry Stapp, Nicholas's commander during the Mexican War.

Though the Wyatt Earp of Western lore was a steadfast lawman who tamed frontier towns, frequently using his gun to do so, historical records do not indicate that he had any need for gunplay in Lamar. On the contrary, the biggest problem facing the city in 1870 was an onslaught of hogs running wild in the streets.

Nonetheless, Earp's appointment was praised in a small page-one item in the *Lamar Southwest Missourian*: "This is a good appointment and when our city dads get the machine in grinding order, law-breakers had better look out. We have some hopes of seeing our public square put and kept in order."

On January 24, 1870, shortly before his appointment as constable, Wyatt Earp married Urilla Sutherland, twenty, daughter of William and Permelia Sutherland. William owned the Exchange Hotel, where the ceremony was performed, with Justice of the Peace Nicholas Earp officiating, something he also did on May 28, 1870, when his son Virgil married Rozella Dragoo.

With Wyatt's starting salary as constable only fifteen dollars a month, the newlyweds lived at her father's hotel until Wyatt was able to save fifty-six dollars and bought a house.

The biggest event in the first few months of Earp's law-enforcement career took place in June 1870, when he arrested three drunken revelers at Elihu Martin's saloon. Unfortunately, one escaped the jail before morning by climbing through a hole in the roof. The other two were fined five dollars each for disturbing the peace.

Only a few months after Earp's appointment as constable, city leaders decided to make it an elected position. Wyatt Earp filed for the position and so did his half brother Newton.

As there did not seem to be any kind of feud within the family (Newton later named one of his sons after Wyatt), historians have speculated that the Earps may have been trying to make sure the job stayed in the family.

In November 1870, Wyatt Earp defeated Newton Earp, 137 to 108. Though Wyatt later gained fame, primarily through TV and movies as a renowned lawman, this was the only time he was elected to office, and he did not hold the office for long.

Shortly after the election, Urilla, who was carrying Wyatt's first child, became ill. Sources differ on the cause of her death, some saying it was due to typhus and others claiming it was during childbirth. The only thing certain was that neither mother nor child survived.

Though a grave in Lamar's East Cemetery has a hand-chiseled inscription, "Mrs. Wyatt Earp," Reba Earp Young, the daughter of Wyatt's brother Johnathon Earp, insisted that a family member had told her Urilla was actually buried in Howell Cemetery in Milford in Barton County.

Wyatt sold the house he had purchased just a few months earlier for seventy-five dollars.

It was not long after Urilla Sutherland Earp's death that Wyatt's time in Lamar came to an end, with his uneventful days as constable suddenly becoming enshrouded in controversy among allegations that the city's law-enforcement officer had stepped over to the other side.

After the untimely death of Urilla, the Sutherland family blamed her death at such an early age on her husband, which led to a brawl that began at Elihu Martin's saloon.

Amanda Cobb, a teenage barmaid in the saloon who later married the owner, said the brawl began in the saloon but did not stay there long.

While Cobb was not certain who started the fight, it pitted Earp and his brothers James, Virgil and Morgan against Urilla's brothers Fred and Bert Sutherland and their friends Granville, Loyd and Jordan Brummett.

Martin, who in addition to owning the saloon served as bartender, bookkeeper and bouncer, kept numerous weapons under the bar and grabbed one of them, a pearl-handled .32-caliber Smith & Wesson revolver, and fired it into the ceiling.

The shot did not stop the fight, but it served its purpose. The men left the saloon and took their battle into the street. As a crowd gathered, the Earp brothers received a beating and were told to get out of town, according to Cobb.

Whether that had anything to do with Earp's subsequent departure is unclear. While Cobb's recollection of the event squared with others, the fight took place weeks before Earp left, indicating that it was not the primary reason he abandoned his first law-enforcement job.

On March 14, 1871, a lawsuit was filed against Earp in Barton County Circuit Court by county officials alleging that he owed $200 in license fees he had collected that were supposed to go into the county's school fund.

Circuit court records indicate that the case against Earp was dismissed because there was no way the money could be collected and that county officials had "good reason to believe and [do] believe that Wyatt S. Earp left, is not a resident of this state, that Wyatt S. Earp has absconded or absented himself from his usual place of abode in this state so that the ordinary process of law cannot be served against him."

Seventeen days after the county's lawsuit was filed, Lamar resident James Cromwell filed a lawsuit claiming that Earp falsified documents and kept a portion of a license fee. According to Cromwell, he had paid the fee, but Earp indicated he was thirty-eight dollars short.

Since Cromwell supposedly had not paid his fee, the county confiscated his mowing machine. Cromwell sued Earp for seventy-five dollars, the value of the machine. The lawsuit met the same fate as the Barton County action. A summons was issued for Earp, but he was never served.

Judge S.J. Bowman decided in favor of Earp, but Cromwell appealed the decision. The judge ruled that the property of Wyatt Earp should be seized to cover Cromwell's cost. Whether Cromwell ever received anything of value to cover his loss is not recorded.

With claims of embezzlement hanging over his head, Earp was long gone from Lamar. On March 28, Earp and two other men, Edward Kennedy and John Shown, were charged with stealing two horses. After the three men were arrested, Kennedy was tried and acquitted. Earp did not wait for trial. Following the example of the drunken reveler he had arrested early in his tenure as Lamar's constable, Earp escaped through a hole in the roof.

Biographers and reporters researching Wyatt Earp during the final years of his life were never able to get him to talk about the short time he spent in Lamar, and Earp also did his best to convince others to close the door on inquiries into that period of his life.

Though Wyatt Earp was no longer in Lamar, many members of his family remained in the city, including some who did a more credible job of enforcing the law than their more famous relative.

One who remained was Wyatt's older brother Johnathon Douglas Earp, a Southern Methodist minister whose son Walter Marvin Earp, Wyatt's cousin, was elected Barton County sheriff and eventually became a well-respected judge.

Walter Earp's son Everett served as one of his deputies.

Known as "Big Chief," Everett Earp had a lengthy career in law enforcement and had the distinction of being Lamar's last constable, just as Wyatt had been the first. Though the opportunities to use the skill were few and far between, Everett Earp also had a reputation for having a quick draw.

He claimed the skill had been passed down through the Earp family and that he passed it on to his son Roy, who later developed a reputation as the fastest draw in the Oakland, California Police Department and was profiled in the *Oakland Tribune*.

None of the Earps who remained in Lamar achieved the fame their cousin Wyatt did, but Judge Walter Earp received nationwide attention following his death in December 1945, when President Harry S. Truman sent a telegram to his family: "I am terribly distressed to hear of the death of your father and my good friend. Please accept the deepest sympathy of Bess and myself in your bereavement."

The future president visited Walter Earp's home on Kentucky Avenue in Lamar on August 31, 1944. It was not the first time Truman had been in the house, though he had no memory of being there before.

Walter Earp's home was the same frame structure where the future president was born on May 8, 1884, and spent the first ten months of his life.

While little has been added to the historical record of Wyatt Earp's brief stay in Lamar, thanks to the limited amount of legal documents and newspaper accounts related to his time as constable, the discovery of a photograph of the legendary lawman taken in January 1870—if authentic, it is the only known photograph in existence of Earp while he was in Lamar—has stirred debate among historians and those with an avid interest in the Old West.

Marshall Bulle, owner of a tool-manufacturing company in Colorado City, Colorado, and a collector of Old West documents and artifacts, purchased the thirty-six-by-twenty-two-inch portrait in 2006 and was initially skeptical that the person in the photograph was Earp and did not begin to investigate its authenticity until 2016, following the airing of a television documentary about efforts to authenticate a purported photo of Billy the Kid.

Bulle and art and antiques dealer Gary Stover began a years-long effort to determine if the man in the photo is Earp, with neither Bulle nor Stover convinced it was authentic.

After their investigation, Bulle and Stover compiled a strong circumstantial case that the photo was authentic, which they spell out in the independently published book *Wyatt Earp (1869–1870): The Lost Story*. In it, Bulle and Stover note that a previous owner of the photo who bought it at auction said the auctioneer had described it as a portrait of Wyatt Earp and that it had been a part of a museum's collection at one time.

Comparing the photo of Earp to photos taken later in his life, the men determined that all of the photos show an identical birthmark on his ear.

This photo of Wyatt Earp, taken by Candace Reed in 1870, was sold at auctions by museum officials as a portrait of Wyatt Earp. If the identification is accurate, it is believed to be the only photo taken of Earp while he was living in Lamar. *Provided by Marshall Bulle.*

Earp relatives claimed the man in the photo was definitely an Earp, because of the downturned corner of his eyes, a result of an uncommon inherited condition known as dermatochalasis.

The men were able to determine that the photo was taken in 1870 at the studio of noted photographer Candace Reed in Quincy, Illinois, and surmised that the photo was likely taken during a bridal tour following the marriage of Wyatt Earp and Urilla Sutherland, which would have taken them to visit relatives in Monmouth, Illinois. Though the photo was far larger than the usual photos from that time, Bulle and Stover found advertisements indicating that Reed had the capability of making photos of that size in 1870.

The men were unable to find a matching photo of Urilla Sutherland Earp, though they found evidence indicating that such a photo existed at one time. As of 2022, they are still searching for the photo and have offered a reward for information on its whereabouts.

THE BIRTH OF HARRY S. TRUMAN

*T*he population of Lamar stood at seven hundred in 1880 according to the census, and the city was a far cry from the wilderness George Ward and Joseph Parry settled thirty years earlier or the community ravaged by William Quantrill in 1862 and 1864.

The square was lined with elm and maple trees, and the streets were covered with gravel, making a visit to the city far more palatable than to similar-sized communities, where a sudden storm could leave streets filled with mud.

Lamar had five churches—Baptist, Christian, Methodist, Presbyterian and Congregational—and a thriving business community complete with livery stables, real estate companies, banks and saloons.

It was a perfect place for a young couple looking to start anew, or so it seemed to John Anderson Truman, thirty-one, a mule and horse trader, and his wife, Martha Ellen (Mattie) Young Truman. They paid $685 to buy the Simon Blethrode house four blocks east of the square on Kentucky Avenue.

The Blethrode property was a corner lot measuring 80 by 150 feet. The small, white frame, two-story house had six rooms, four downstairs and two upstairs. The home had no basement, attic or clothes closet, and the bathroom, as it was in most houses at that time, was in a separate wood building constructed specifically for that purpose. The deed was recorded on November 14, 1882, at the Barton County Courthouse. Truman paid an additional $200 for a barn across the street, where he established his mule and horse-trading business.

When the Trumans arrived, Mattie Truman was pregnant with their first child. The child was stillborn on October 25, 1882.

John Truman's business struggled, and on June 20, 1883, he took out an advertisement on page one of the *Lamar Democrat*: "Mules bought and sold. I will keep for sale at the White Barn on Kentucky Avenue a lot of good mules. Anyone wanting teams will do well to call on J.A. Truman."

It was not long before the Trumans had a second chance at parenthood. On May 7, 1884, what was described as a "baby cyclone" hit the Lamar area, according to the *Democrat*, which described an active day in the city. The newspaper carried little of what would be called news today but offered a full assessment of what Lamar's businesses had to offer, mixed with observations about politics and the weather.

According to the May 8, 1884 edition, Cunningham Drug Store was offering a new miracle cure, Papillon Skin Care—"a specific cure for all skin diseases, salt rheum, rash, inflammation, insect bites, inordinate itching, ulcers, cuts, wounds, burns or scales and scrofulous eruptions [inflammation of the eyes and ears]."

Byrd's Ice Cream Parlor advertised that it was "neat, clean and cozy," was newly remodeled and "is the place to bring your girl." The Palace Barber Shop and Bath Room offered "shaving, hair cutting and shampooing with ease and celerity" and promised not to charge anything if the customer was not satisfied.

The big news was that J.M. Fisher bought "Prince, the Roadster Stallion, a beautiful bay with black points, six years old, 16 hands high and weighs 1,200 pounds of fine style and good action and is among the best bred stallions in the southwest."

The *Lamar Democrat* of May 8, 1884, missed the most newsworthy item that occurred that day, the birth of a future president of the United States, though the child's father was once again featured in a page-one advertisement: "Wanted a few good mules and horses. Will pay highest cash prices for same. J.A. Truman, White Barn near Missouri Pacific Depot."

The extra business would come in handy, as the Truman family had an extra mouth to feed as of that day. Dr. William L. Griffin, who sported a distinguished thatch of white hair with a long, flowing beard, rode what he claimed to be "the fastest horse in Barton County" to the Truman home and delivered the baby in a downstairs room measuring six feet, six inches by ten feet, nine inches.

Griffin, whose office was three blocks northeast of the square, was a physician, surgeon and obstetrician who paid special attention to chronic diseases. For the task of delivering a future president, the Trumans paid Griffin fifteen dollars.

John Truman commemorated the birth of his son by planting a pine tree beside the home and, legend has it, nailed a mule shoe above the door for good luck. After debating what name to give their child, the Trumans named him Harry, after his uncle Harrison Young, and gave him the middle initial *S* in honor of his grandfathers, Solomon Young and Anderson Shippe Truman.

On June 5, 1884, Dr. Griffin recorded on the birth certificate that a son had been born on May 8 to John and Martha Truman, their ages and John's occupation. The one thing that was not recorded on the certificate was the baby's name. That was added six decades later.

Harry S. Truman lived in Lamar for only the first ten months of his life. With his mule business failing, John Truman sold the home and barn for $1,600, and the family moved to Harrisonville. It would be another thirty-nine years before Harry Truman returned to the city where he was born.

ARTHUR AULL

*I*n the late 1800s, while newspapers featured some community news and carried advertising from local businesses, many were created solely to serve political parties.

Lee Chiswell, a rising star in Barton County Democratic circles and considered to be a candidate for statewide office, was elected prosecuting attorney at the age of twenty-four. After serving ten years in that office, Chiswell surprised local Democrats when he opted not to run for reelection. Instead, the Maryland native intended to concentrate on his law practice and try his hand at something new.

In 1882, Chiswell bought the *Barton County Progress* and the following year renamed it the *Lamar Democrat*.

Chiswell used his newspaper to support the Democratic Party and developed an avid readership in Barton County with his whimsical writing and sly sense of humor.

In the May 8, 1884 edition of the *Democrat*, Chiswell wrote the following about a visitor to Lamar: "Bill Moody is in town. It seems that he was asked to leave Appleton City and remain away 12 months. He married an overconfiding girl and then mistreated her. The girl's father clubbed him and finally shot at him. He was arrested and fined five dollars for not hitting him."

Over the next several years, Chiswell was a successful newspaperman, investing money in modern equipment that was described in the December 20, 1892 *Springfield News* as "the most complete and convenient printing machines of the present time."

Shown here is a young Arthur Aull. Lamar Democrat.

In November 1895, Chiswell suffered a stroke and stepped down as editor. A month later, he suffered another stroke, and on May 2, 1897, a third stroke caused the death of Chiswell at age forty-nine.

The newspaper Chiswell steered to local prominence suffered under new leadership and was in danger of shutting down when new ownership put the *Lamar Democrat* on a path to being a newspaper with a national readership.

The new owner, Arthur Fabian Aull, was born on November 18, 1872, in Kentucky and moved to a farm in Nashville Township in western Barton County with his father and stepmother when he was twelve. Aull, an industrious young man, not only did chores on the family farm but also worked as a hired hand on nearby farms, using the money he received to buy books. His plan was to study law. He attended Fort Scott, Kansas Normal College for two years. Aull took a teaching position at the Nashville Township school he had attended only a few years earlier and studied law in the evening.

During that time, Aull courted a young Lamar woman, Luanna Turnbull, also a teacher, who shared Aull's love of reading. As Turnbull was taking a teaching position at the Nashville school, Aull accepted a higher-paying position as superintendent of the Mindenmines School District in western Barton County.

Arthur Aull and Luanna Turnbull were married on March 22, 1896, in Nashville, and three years later, Aull came home with news for his wife.

"He heard that the *Lamar Democrat* was for sale again," Luanna Aull recalled in an article she wrote for the newspaper in 1957. She was skeptical of the idea but changed her mind after her husband convinced a Lamar banker to loan him the $6,000 he needed to buy the newspaper.

In August 1900, Arthur Aull became owner, publisher and editor of the *Lamar Democrat*. Though he had never considered a career in journalism, Aull immediately fell in love with the news. The new owner had a curiosity about everything. He wrote about agriculture, business, social events, crime and anything else that interested him.

Aull's daily rounds began with a shave at the barbershop. He then went to city hall, schools, churches, the jail, hospitals, funeral homes, businesses on the square and the Barton County Courthouse.

Arthur Aull at his desk. Lamar Democrat.

It was at the courthouse that Aull gathered detailed information about anything that took place in criminal and civil cases. With no formal training in journalism, Aull determined that he would print the complete truth, and that is exactly what he did—at least his version of it.

He wrote detailed descriptions of contested divorces that scandalized the community but kept the readers coming back for more. The stories were invariably written from the point of view of the party suing for divorce, such as in the following: "She had an awful temper, he said, and would fly into a rage upon the most trivial occasion. She told him she didn't love him. She wouldn't cook his meals, nor keep the house in order. She took night rides with other men and let them take indecent liberties with her. When he protested, she told him she would do as she pleased and for him to go to hell."

Aull offered gory descriptions of accidents and crime scenes. Year after year, decade after decade, Aull's no-holds-barred brand of journalism entertained and occasionally angered readers, but they always knew what was happening in Lamar, with no details omitted.

The *Democrat* became a daily publication in 1904, with Aull writing every word of the newspaper every day. Competitors were never able to keep up

Arthur Aull in front of the
Lamar Democrat with his dog
Tippy in the early 1940s.
Lamar Democrat.

with the onslaught of words Aull issued, nor were they willing to provide the kind of stories he was publishing.

Aull had been the editor of the *Democrat* for more than thirty years when he reached a level of success he had never believed possible. His detailed articles caught the eye of Ted Cook, a *Los Angeles Examiner* humor columnist whose work was syndicated in hundreds of newspapers through Hearst.

Cook began using Aull's writing as fodder for his columns. Subsequently, readers across the United States decided they wanted to subscribe to the *Lamar Democrat*. Among the new subscribers was movie star and comedian W.C. Fields.

At that point, with few people aware of Wyatt Earp's connection and with Harry S. Truman representing Missouri in the U.S. Senate, Arthur Aull was the most famous person to come from Lamar.

4

JAY LYNCH

*O*ne of the most sordid chapters in Lamar history began when a wanted criminal from the St. Louis area decided to evade capture by taking an assumed name and staying with relatives in the Verdella area of Barton County.

Josiah "Jay" Lynch Jr. was born in 1889 in Rich Hill, Missouri, the youngest of three children of Josiah and Maude Lynch. By the time he arrived in Barton County in 1919, he had a lengthy history of criminal activity, including arrests for robbery and burglary. He had enlisted in the U.S. Navy twice, once under an assumed name, and had been court-martialed both times.

Despite his crimes, the Wabash Railroad hired Lynch as a detective in 1918, and he repaid them by stealing items from freight cars. After he was arrested at his sister's Barton County home, Lynch was taken to the Barton County Jail in Lamar, where he was to be held until he could be returned to St. Louis to stand trial.

As Sheriff John Harlow prepared to take him to St. Louis, Lynch asked if he could phone his wife, who was staying with his sister. Harlow gave him permission to use a phone in the hallway.

Arthur Aull described what happened next in an article in the March 6, 1919 *Lamar Democrat*:

> *As Lynch ceased to talk, he suddenly whipped a revolver from his clothes, no one knows just where, pointed it at the sheriff and told him to put up his hands. Then Lynch opened fire. One bullet struck the sheriff in the left*

breast, a short distance above the nipple, was deflected by a rib, went out the left side of his chest and grazed the arm.

Lynch continued to fire, with a second bullet hitting the sheriff only a few inches from where the first had landed. Since the sheriff's family was having its evening meal in a separate area of the building, which also included the Harlows' home, John Harlow's wife was only a short distance from her husband when he died.

Their son Walter Forrest Harlow—called "Dick" by the family—had just returned home. He heard the shots, ran into the building and became the second victim. Lynch felled the younger Harlow with one shot. He was clinging to life as Lynch escaped.

It took several hours for Lynch to get away from Lamar, since he was generally unfamiliar with the wooded areas outside of the city. He became lost and traveled about seven and a half miles, but being unfamiliar with Lamar, he found himself two blocks from where he had started. Lynch watched as law-enforcement officers, accompanied by bloodhounds brought in from Carthage and Springfield, hunted for him.

Lynch eventually escaped Missouri and made his way to La Junta, Colorado, where he was captured on May 13, 1919, and extradited to Missouri.

During Sheriff John Harlow's funeral, his widow was called away when her son, who had been in a Carthage hospital since the shooting, took a turn for the worse. He died later that day, adding a second murder victim to Lynch's toll.

The capture of Jay Lynch occurred after another wanted man nearly took his place in the Barton County Jail.

During the time the manhunt for Lynch was in full swing, a small-time crook named Frank O'Mara, who bore a striking resemblance to Lynch, was arrested near Carthage, twenty-five miles south of Lamar. O'Mara, who was fully aware of the murders Lynch had committed and knew that Lamar residents were considering vigilante justice to avenge the sheriff, tried desperately to convince Jasper County deputies he was not the man they were seeking.

"I knew what was awaiting Lynch at Lamar and I did not care to be taken there and lynched." O'Mara initially used a fake name but eventually opted to tell the officers he was actually a wanted criminal in Kansas.

"Five years in Lansing was better than five minutes in Lamar," O'Mara said.

Barton County officials confirmed the man being held in the Jasper County Jail was not Lynch.

With the community hungering for vengeance, Sheriff Harlow's replacement, William A. Sewell, had Lynch kept at the Bates County Jail in Butler until the trial and said he feared "no difficulty" in returning Lynch to Lamar when the time came, adding that the bitter feeling had died down.

Sewell was quoted in the May 22, 1919 *Butler Weekly Times and Bates County Record* as saying he could "control my people."

As a precaution, the day of Lynch's hearing, May 28, 1919, was kept secret except from those who needed to be there. But someone leaked the information, and as the time for the hearing approached, a crowd numbering approximately one thousand gathered around the Barton County Courthouse.

Two years earlier, the Missouri legislature had outlawed capital punishment, meaning the most severe sentence Lynch could receive was life in prison—not enough for the gathering mob.

A Vernon County deputy posted outside the courthouse did nothing to discourage the mob, according to a *Kansas City Times* account. "If you fellows don't hang Lynch, we'll get him in Nevada [the Vernon County seat]. Then we will come down and paint your courthouse yellow."

Sheriff Sewell, his deputies and sheriffs and deputies from Bates and Vernon Counties were able to slip Lynch into the courthouse. As the hearing began, Prosecuting Attorney H.W. Timmons read the charges against him. The judge asked how Lynch pleaded. "Guilty," he said in a barely audible voice, causing Judge B.G. Thurman to ask, "Guilty?"

"Yes, but I didn't intend to kill the sheriff. I don't remember having killed his son. It was an accident."

A jury had been impaneled, but Lynch's plea made it unnecessary. After the judge sentenced Lynch to life in prison, he was taken to the judge's chambers to await transfer to the state penitentiary.

A voice called out in the courtroom, "String him up."

Sewell responded, "Someone is going to get arrested."

As officers stood outside and inside the judge's chambers, Lynch was allowed to meet with his mother, Maude Lynch, his sister Stella and his wife, twenty-three-year-old Lola Lynch, who was holding their three-month-old baby.

Jay Lynch's handcuffs were removed so he could hold the baby as he talked with family members. Outside, the mob, whose leader was described as a "well known businessman," began to move toward the courtroom.

Approximately fifty people rushed the judge's chambers. Lola Lynch described the scene. "When we heard the angry shouts of the crowd and saw men spring upon the officers who were guarding the door, Jay handed me my baby daughter and turned to face the men."

The mob pushed aside the officers and entered the room. Sewell, aiming his gun at them, jumped in front of the leader. Sewell was pushed aside, and no shots were fired.

As the mob approached her husband, Lola Lynch fainted and the baby fell out of her arms, but someone alertly caught the child before she hit the floor. Someone struck Lynch in the head with a stone, knocking him unconscious. A rope was placed around his neck.

The mob dragged Lynch through the courtroom, over chairs and other furniture, then out of the courthouse with Lynch's head banging against each of the stone steps. Lynch never regained consciousness and may have already been dead. He was taken to an elm tree, which, coincidentally had been planted by the murder victim Sheriff John Harlow ten years earlier.

The first attempt to hang Jay Lynch was unsuccessful, as the rope slid off Lynch and he slumped to the ground. The mob that watched as the act of vigilante justice occurred before their eyes included women and children. One of the women was Sheriff Harlow's widow. It was her first appearance in public since leaving her husband's funeral.

The second attempt to hang Lynch was successful. Lynch's body remained hanging from the tree for the next few hours as Lamar funeral homes refused to have anything to do with preparing him for burial. Finally, a funeral home in Joplin, forty miles south of Lamar, agreed to take Lynch.

Lola, apparently trying to comfort herself, told a reporter she thought her husband died of a heart attack before the mob was able to hurt him and said it "probably is best as it is. They can't torture him any longer."

Jay Lynch's family accompanied his body to Joplin, where a funeral home prepared it. Dozens of people gathered at the funeral home, hoping to see the killer's body, but funeral officials, respecting the widow's wishes, turned them away. Arrangements were made to bury Lynch in an unmarked grave in Forest Park Cemetery in Joplin.

Though Lynch's family had already left Joplin, a brief ceremony was held later that day, with Reverend E.H. Sapp telling the few who attended that "the wages of sin is death."

The murder of Harlow and another sheriff in 1919 convinced the Missouri legislature to reinstate the death penalty six weeks after Lynch's hanging. A third sheriff, Vernon County sheriff Vern Dawes, one of those who was overpowered while trying to protect Lynch, was murdered on July 18, 1919, while conducting a search of a man who had been brought into the Vernon County Jail. The man pulled a hidden gun and shot Dawes in the heart, killing him instantly.

The lynching of Jay Lynch brought unfavorable national attention to Lamar, including a page-one article in the May 29, 1919 *New York Times*.

Following Lynch's death, officials promised that those who were involved in the vigilante action would be arrested.

Barton County prosecuting attorney H.W. Timmons said he saw a returned soldier climb the tree with the rope and told reporters he had the names of eight other men who were involved in the hanging. His indecision was notable in a quote printed in the June 12, 1919 *Cassville Republican*. "But I am in a quandary how to proceed," Timmons said, "as public sentiment is running high in sympathy with the outrage and having gone through a very strenuous day and night, I have hardly had time to collect my thoughts."

Though Barton County officials insisted that those who were involved in the lynching would be punished, a coroner's inquest determined that Jay Lynch's death came "at the hands of parties unknown."

Stories circulated over the years that prominent Lamar residents had been involved in Lynch's killing, but those names were never revealed. It was the one time in the forty-eight years Arthur Aull published the *Lamar Democrat* that he did not offer complete details on an infamous crime that took place in Lamar.

Jay Lynch's body was removed from Forest Park Cemetery in 1927 and reburied in a family plot in Mount Moriah Cemetery in Kansas City.

THE EARP FAMILY BUYS
THE TRUMAN BIRTHPLACE

*T*hough Lamar's first constable, Wyatt Earp, left the city under suspicious circumstances in 1871, Earp family members remained in the Lamar area, including Wyatt's brother Johnathon Douglas Earp and his family.

Johnathon Earp's son Walter, rather than following in his father's footsteps, claimed the heritage of his cousin Wyatt and his uncles, first becoming a lawman and later a judge.

Walter Earp married Emma Ophelia Hudson, who went by the name Emily, on April 13, 1879, and the couple raised eleven children on acreage east of Lamar on Highway 160.

When Emily's health began to fail in 1920, the Earps left their country home and moved into Lamar, buying a two-story white frame house on Kentucky Avenue. The home did not have any particular historical significance at that point, but it was the same home in which Harry S. Truman had been born thirty-six years earlier.

The appearance of the home had changed since John and Martha Truman owned it. Reba Earp Young, the daughter of Walter and Emily Earp's oldest son, William Buford Earp, and Pearl Mary Earp, described the changes in her 1993 book *Down Memory Lane*, noting that a porch had been built in front of the house and a kitchen added on the northwest corner.

With Emily Earp's health deteriorating, Reba and her sisters stayed with the couple and helped with chores. "We washed many tubs of clothes on the board and did the big baskets of ironing, also, we scrubbed the floor—the very floors the Trumans walked on. We even helped grandmother make her preserves and jellies."

Seventy years after staying in the house, Reba Earp recalled that a fence had been added and the Earps kept a cow on the property so they would have a steady supply of milk, a practice that was not uncommon at the time.

Emily Earp died on February 15, 1923, in the same room where Harry Truman was born thirty-nine years earlier. Her funeral was held in the house. Walter Earp remained in the home for the remaining twenty-two years of his life.

The significance of Harry Truman's birth at that location was first noted in 1934, during Truman's first campaign for U.S. Senate. In a 1944 letter to the *Lamar Democrat,* James H. Lillard of Lamar noted that he had been with a group that escorted Truman; his wife, Bess; their daughter, Margaret; and Truman's mother, Martha Ellis Young Truman, "to what is now the Walter Earp home on East Eleventh Street and Kentucky Avenue. Judge Truman's mother recognized it as her former home."

Truman returned to the house where he was born once again when he came to Lamar for his vice-presidential acceptance speech on August 31, 1944. After the death of President Franklin D. Roosevelt in April 1945, when Truman was sworn in as the thirty-third president of the United States, Lamar received a new round of attention from newspapers and magazines that wanted to find out everything it could about the new commander in chief.

A *Life* magazine article published on June 25, 1945, not only focused the spotlight on the little house on Kentucky Avenue but also created many of the legends that have long been associated with the Truman birthplace.

The *Life* article contained inaccuracies, beginning with the idea that John Truman, who had to leave Lamar in 1885 because his mule business had been unsuccessful, was a slick mule trader. The article indicated that Harry spent the first few years of his life in Lamar, though the family left before his first birthday.

The article featured photos of the home, as well as of Judge Walter Earp and his son Everett. A photo prominently showed a mule shoe that supposedly was the one John Truman nailed above the door after his son was born, though it seems unlikely that all of the home's owners during the sixty-one years since the Trumans left would have kept the mule shoe above the door.

Walter Earp's relation to Wyatt Earp, who by this time was becoming a symbol of the lawmen who had tamed the West, was highlighted in the article. Walter did not have much time to enjoy his newly found fame. He died on December 21, 1945, at age eighty-seven.

With his father's death, Everett Earp became owner of the Truman birthplace and determined that the house should become a monument to President Truman. And if Earp could make some money along the way, he had no problem with that.

Earp tried to convince city officials to put a sign in his yard noting that the home was where Truman was born. When city officials rejected his request, Earp put a prominent sign in front of the house: "Harry S. Truman, President of the United States was born here—Everett Earp, owner." He nailed a sign advertising his real estate business to the pine tree John Truman planted the day his son was born.

When visitors began to come to the house, Earp charged them fifty cents for a tour, though he insisted he wasn't charging admission. He said he gave visitors cards and asked for fifty cents.

Earp contacted state officials in 1948 to gauge their interest in buying the home. They were interested enough to have the property appraised. The results were not what Everett was expecting. The property was appraised at $750, only $65 more than John Truman had paid Simon Blethrode in 1882.

State officials were willing to go above that figure, with the backing of the legislature, all the way to $15,000, but Earp would not settle for a penny less than $30,000. When Earp realized he was not going to get what he hoped for, he brought the price down to $25,000, but that was still far more than state officials were willing to pay.

Earp continued to make money giving tours as long as Truman was in the White House, but once the Eisenhower administration was in place in 1953, the number making the pilgrimage to Lamar dwindled and the stories Earp told visitors strayed further from the truth.

Earp's tall tales were evident in syndicated columnist Helen Worden Erskine's account of a November 1955 visit to the home. While Earp sat in a rocking chair in front of a fire, he told Erskine, "My pappy bought it from Harry's father." In reality, Walter Earp did not buy the property until 1920, thirty-five years after John Truman left Lamar.

"We make enough showing it summers to feed us winters," Earp said, adding that even if he was not able to make enough money giving the tours, he would continue to give them.

"I'm proud to have folks see where a president of the United States was born." Earp said he hoped the city of Lamar would keep the home as a museum after he died. Earp took Erskine to the room where Mattie Truman gave birth to the future president. "On a bed like this, in this here spot, is where Harry Truman was born. My pappy saw him when he was a mighty puny baby, only eight hours old."

Earp did not confine his remarks to Truman but brought his own relative into the conversation, pointing out an article on Wyatt Earp. "Wyatt was my cousin. I've been a two-gun sheriff. It runs in the family. My boy's a two-gun sheriff in California."

At that point, Earp brought the conversation back to Truman and referenced a November 1, 1950 assassination attempt by Puerto Rican pro-independence activists Oscar Collazo and Griselio Torresola. "When them Puerto Rican desperadoes started shootin' at Harry that time in Washington me and my boy said, 'What Harry needs is us.'"

During the first week of November 1956, Everett Earp suffered a stroke. He died on November 8, 1956, at age seventy-four in the house where Truman was born.

On April 30, 1957, Earp's widow, Marie, sold the house to the United Auto Workers (UAW) for $6,000. Officials in the Kansas City and St. Louis locals of the UAW had heard reports that the house was deteriorating and wanted to do something to show their appreciation to Truman for contributions he had made to the cause of organized labor.

UAW officials planned to restore the home on Kentucky Avenue, making it look the way it did on May 8, 1884. After that, they would present it to the state of Missouri to become a shrine for Harry Truman.

6

H.C. CHANCELLOR

Though the name Henry Columbus Chancellor, more commonly referred to as "H.C.," is not familiar today in Lamar, the contributions he made to the city are still evident, including the miniature Statue of Liberty that stands on the courthouse grounds, the concrete highway U.S. 160 from Lamar to the Missouri-Kansas state line and, most important, Barton County Memorial Hospital, now known as Cox Barton County Hospital.

H.C. was the oldest son of Henry Clay Chancellor, who was born on May 8, 1847, in Clark County, Illinois. The elder Chancellor's father died at a young age, and Henry, fifteen, with the permission of his uncle and guardian Joshua Chancellor, enlisted in the Union army, where he participated in the Battle of Perryville and in General William Sherman's march to the sea. He suffered a serious shoulder wound during the siege of Atlanta.

After the war, Henry Chancellor married Sarah Jane Bowen, who gave birth to H.C. on January 2, 1868. Shortly after that, the Chancellors moved to Arcadia, Kansas, thirty miles west of Lamar. As Chancellor reached adulthood, he, like Arthur Aull, took teaching positions in rural Barton County schools.

Tragedy was no stranger to Chancellor, whose first wife died in childbirth. In 1893, he wed a second time, to Susie Christenson, a visitor from Bicknell, Indiana. The couple moved to Bicknell, where Chancellor established the city's first newspaper, the weekly *Bicknell Bulletin*.

Four years later, Susie Chancellor was stricken with tuberculosis. For a second time, Chancellor was a widower. This time, he was a widower with a one-year-old daughter. A year after his wife's death, Chancellor married Pearl Victoria Freeman, sold the *Bulletin* and returned to Barton County.

Chancellor operated a loan and insurance business in Minden and organized the Bank of Minden and the Minden Telephone Company. For the next thirty years, he divided his time between his businesses and serving three terms in the Missouri House of Representatives (1907–8, 1917–18 and 1919–20). In his second term, Chancellor led an effort for construction of rural roads across the state, including several in Barton County.

In Chancellor's third term, he was already sponsoring legislation to restore the death penalty in Missouri when Jay Lynch was hanged on the Barton County Courthouse grounds. The legislation passed shortly after the hanging.

H.C. and Pearl Chancellor had four children, Harold, Marguerite, Richard and Crystal; the latter died of whooping cough when she was nine months old.

In 1929, Chancellor sold the Bank of Minden and, three years later, at age sixty-four, moved into Lamar and bought the Travelers Hotel, a half-block south of the square.

The Travelers Hotel opened as the McMillen Hotel during the Christmas holiday season in 1897. Within a year, it was sold and became the Jackson Hotel, which it remained until 1916, when it was sold. After a third sale two years later, the name was changed to the Hotel Travelers, eventually becoming the Travelers Hotel.

Chancellor managed the hotel for the next dozen years before handing the reins over to his son Harold Chancellor. During the Chancellors' ownership of the Travelers, it became the leading hotel in Lamar. Many of the city's major events were held there, including perhaps the biggest event in Lamar history: the return of Harry S. Truman to accept the vice-presidential nomination on August 31, 1944.

H.C.'s efforts were not limited to running the hotel. He continued to work for the community, leading a successful effort to have concrete installed and U.S. 160 improved from Lamar to the Missouri-Kansas state line.

Even after Chancellor was no longer running the hotel, he continued to be active in the community, saving his greatest contribution until near the end of his life.

In 1944, as World War II was coming to a close, the Jesse C. Rains American Legion Post 209 of Lamar proposed building a memorial to Barton County boys who had lost their lives. After hearing of their plan, Chancellor, whose son Richard was being held as a prisoner of war, suggested a memorial that could mean much more to Lamar and Barton County. Since the county did not have a hospital, Chancellor suggested the idea that eventually became Barton County Memorial Hospital.

Chancellor was named head of the hospital committee and led efforts to land dual sources for the money needed to make the building a reality. He hoped to receive state funding, but most of the project's cost would be financed through a bond issue. County voters had to be convinced to reach into their pockets to build the hospital.

With Chancellor leading the drive, Barton County voters not only approved the $100,000 bond issue on February 19, 1946, but also approved it overwhelmingly, 3,047 to 272. The margin was even bigger in Lamar, which approved the measure 1,416 to 25.

Eventually, when the state did not come through with as much money as Chancellor and the committee hoped and a government grant fell through, Barton County voters had to approve a second bond issue and did, though the margin was somewhat smaller.

A dedication for Barton County Memorial Hospital was held on October 1, 1949, but only nine days earlier, the *Joplin Globe* had reported that Chancellor, eighty, was "severely ill from a heart ailment." He resigned as head of the committee and was replaced by his son Harold.

A flag-raising ceremony was held, and a plaque with the names of the sixty-nine Barton County soldiers who died during the war was unveiled.

On May 22, 1951, H C. Chancellor died in the hospital that existed only through his efforts.

RICHARD CHANCELLOR

At the time H.C. Chancellor launched the drive to establish Barton County Memorial Hospital as a tribute to the soldiers who lost their lives overseas, he had to wonder if the name of one of his children would be among those who would be honored.

Richard Freeman Chancellor, born on November 3, 1917, in Mindenmines, worked during his teen years for his father at the Travelers Hotel and dreamed of becoming a pilot. After graduating from Lamar High School in 1935, Richard attended Kemper Military Academy in Boonville for two years and completed three years at the Rolla School of Mines.

In early 1941, as the United States prepared for what appeared to be its inevitable entry into World War II, Richard Chancellor was the second man from Barton County to be drafted. The community held a rally for the first man drafted, including a performance by the Lamar High School Band. Unfortunately, the man failed his physical at Fort Leavenworth. No such celebration was held for Chancellor, who took a 3:00 a.m. bus for his physical, with only his mother, Pearl Chancellor, to see him off.

Chancellor was initially assigned to the First Armored Unit at Fort Knox, which was sent with other units to conduct field maneuvers in July 1941, first in Louisiana, then in southern Arkansas and finally in the Carolinas.

After months of maneuvers, the soldiers returned to Fort Knox on December 7, 1941. As they were unloading their trucks and taking their personal gear into the barracks, they received word that Pearl Harbor had been attacked.

"It was a shock to all of us and especially to those of us who were draftees as we were nearing the end of our mandatory year of service and were looking forward to getting out," Chancellor wrote in the 1990s.

All leaves were canceled and training intensified. Chancellor spotted a bulletin board notice that the U.S. Army Air Corps would be conducting interviews with those who wanted to join combat crews. He was accepted and received his flight training at Parks Air College in St. Louis. He quickly distinguished himself as an excellent pilot and leader of men and completed numerous successful missions before encountering a perilous situation on September 15, 1943, when his plane experienced mechanical difficulties following a bombing mission over southern Italy as it was returning to the base after bombing a railroad junction in Potanza.

After determining that repairs could not be made, Lieutenant Chancellor told his crew they would have to ride the plane to the ground and hope for the best. The plane crashed into the water. Noticing that two of his men were unable to exit the plane, Chancellor dived into the water and rescued both of them, one of whom had suffered a broken neck.

Eight of the eleven men in the plane survived. With the few provisions they had, they crawled into two life rafts. At one point, they narrowly avoided being spotted by a German U-boat. After a few days at sea, during which time Chancellor and his men were reported missing in action, they were rescued.

When Chancellor returned to the states in February 1944, a ceremony was held awarding him a medal for "bravery beyond the call of duty" for rescuing the two soldiers who had been trapped in the plane wreckage.

After the award ceremony, Chancellor returned to Europe. Five months later, during the return trip after flying a successful mission on July 22, 1944, the engines on Chancellor's bomber were struck by ground fire, forcing him to crash land in Yugoslavia.

Though Chancellor and his crew survived, he suffered a severely broken arm, as well as other minor injuries. His men sustained cuts and bruises.

Within a short time, they were taken prisoner and transported to Sarajevo. From there, they were taken to Stalag Luft III in Poland, a POW camp for captured airmen.

While the men were treated far better by their Luftwaffe guards than those held in other prisons, life was still difficult. The meals varied little and offered almost no nutritional value. They usually comprised "a daily portion of German bread and cabbage soup," Chancellor said. A loaf of bread weighed four pounds, and the prisoners often received only 1/12 of a loaf.

Though the cabbage soup's taste was not unpleasant, Chancellor said, it came nowhere near meeting the prisoners' appetites, and it often came garnished, unintentionally, with fresh maggots.

In addition to hunger, Chancellor had to deal with the effects of his broken shoulder. The camp's doctors had never dealt with the kind of complex fracture he had suffered. One operation failed, and the doctors tried another. Chancellor, having heard stories of Nazi atrocities, was left to wonder what was being done to him. "Richard thought the doctors were conducting experiments on him," his wife, Ione, recalled in a 2019 interview. The doctors' efforts left Chancellor in constant pain.

When the camp was liberated in January 1945, Chancellor was no longer there, as he had begun the first of two forced marches. During the marches, the airmen not only had to deal with the bitter winter cold but also risked death from friendly fire from Allied bombers.

During one such instance, Chancellor found himself dodging bullets and dived into a trench to avoid bombs. He found himself with another prisoner, a young man named Bill Goade, who, coincidentally, was from Duenweg, Missouri, a town three miles east of Joplin and approximately forty miles from Lamar.

In late May 1945, H.C. and Pearl Chancellor received word from the War Department that their son had been freed and was back in the United States. On June 2, the family was reunited. Three weeks later, Richard Chancellor and the sweetheart he had left behind, Ione Williams, were married in the Chancellor home at 209 South Gulf Street.

After his return to civilian life, Chancellor worked for his brother Harold at the Travelers Hotel and then briefly ran a successful hardware store on the Lamar Square, but he remained restless. The leadership skills he had honed during his years in the service were not being used, and he wanted to do something more with his life.

Eventually, Chancellor became a top official with the city's biggest employer, Lawn-Boy, and later became president of Barton County State Bank. He served two terms on the Lamar City Council before his death in 2000 at age eighty-two.

8
HISTORY REPEATS ITSELF

*T*wenty-five years after the murders of Barton County sheriff John Harlow and his son Dick during Jay Lynch's escape from the Barton County Jail in Lamar, history repeated itself in a horrific way when yet another Barton County sheriff and his son were murdered.

The events leading to the deaths of Sheriff Roy Patterson and his son Sammie began at Hite's Phillips 66 truck stop in Jasper, Missouri, twelve miles south of Lamar.

Situated on busy Highway 71 at a time when one could take a trip on the highways of America and be able to see a city without taking an off-ramp, Hite's was a regular stop for drivers, especially truckers, who needed gasoline, a sandwich, a piece of pie and a cup of coffee before returning to the road.

At 2:30 a.m. on August 17, 1944, the only people at Hite's were night attendant Pearce Hastings and sixteen-year-old waitress Lilly Bemis. Three men entered and ordered coffee. Two of them stood about six feet tall, the other a few inches shorter. They appeared to be in their early to mid-twenties,

When Bemis returned with the coffee, she found one of the men pointing a .32-caliber pistol in her direction. Another wielded a long-barreled weapon and trained it on Hastings.

The third man opened the cash register and removed between $130.00 and $140.00 and gas-rationing stamps and forced Hastings to hand over his wallet, which contained $29.59. The man with the rifle took Hastings out to their black Ford and had him fill up the tank with about $8.00 worth of gasoline. Moments later, the three men drove away from Hite's and headed north on Highway 71.

As soon as he could get back into the building, Hastings phoned Barton County sheriff Roy Patterson at his home, filled him in on the robbery and let him know the men were headed in his direction.

Patterson, who was exhausted after driving to and from Springfield the previous day, asked his son Sammie if he would drive and told him to "get the guns."

Ira Farmer, who raised cattle on land about a mile west of Lamar, was awakened at 4:00 a.m. by a series of loud noises he thought sounded like a car backfiring. When he stepped outside to investigate, he saw two parked cars and, a few moments later, one of the cars heading east at a high rate of speed. He went back into his house.

At daybreak, after eating breakfast, he tended his cattle and saw that the other car was still there with the passenger side door open and a man's legs hanging out.

Figuring the man was sleeping, Farmer continued his chores, but when he finished, the car was still there and the man's legs were still hanging out, appearing to be in the same position they were earlier.

When Farmer checked, he discovered the blood-soaked bodies of Roy and Sammie Patterson. Roy's feet were on the ground, with the upper portion of his body on the seat. Sammie's head was slumped over the steering wheel; his foot was on the brake.

Farmer ran into his house and called Raymond River, owner of River Funeral Home and the Barton County coroner. River contacted Patterson's chief deputy, Joshua Box. Within ten minutes, River and deputies were on the scene.

Roy Patterson's gun was empty; the other weapon, a shotgun, had not been fired. The killer shot the sheriff three times, one of the bullets hitting him in the back of the neck and exiting just below his eye. He had also been shot in the right ear.

Sammie Patterson, who had been unarmed, was shot once, the fatal bullet hitting him just below the left ear.

The coroner's inquest into the Pattersons' murders had just begun at River Funeral Home on Friday, August 18, and the first witness had been called when a message was delivered to River that he was needed at the scene of an accident just past the railroad tracks on the eastern edge of the city limits.

When River arrived, he found the body of five-year-old Bonnie Kay Millard on the street by Brasher's filling station, which was owned by Bonnie's grandparents Mr. and Mrs. J.E. Brasher.

The child and her seven-year-old sister had been walking along Highway 160 when they were struck by a seventeen-year-old driver who later told police he had to drive toward the side of the road to avoid a head-on collision with another vehicle.

Bonnie Kay Millard suffered a broken neck and died before a doctor could arrive. Her sister, who had her arm around Bonnie Kay when the car struck her, suffered a bruised arm and hand.

The inquest into the Pattersons' deaths resumed when River returned. Witnesses included Sheriff Patterson's widow; Ira Farmer, who discovered the bodies; the doctor who performed the autopsies; and interim sheriff Joshua Box.

Two witnesses who had been scheduled to testify, sixteen-year-old waitress Lilly Bemis and night attendant Pearce Hastings from Hite's Phillips 66 in Jasper, did not testify.

Bemis and Hastings were in Skiatook, Oklahoma, to identify two suspects who had been taken into custody. The men, along with another man, had escaped from an Oklahoma prison and fit the descriptions of the men suspected of robbing Hite's and killing the Pattersons. The other man had been captured and was being held in another location. The two men were not the ones who robbed Hite's Phillips 66 and killed the sheriff and his son.

The funeral of Roy and Sammie Patterson was held on August 22, 1944, at Memorial Hall. A large building for a city the size of Lamar, it was inadequate to handle the number of people who came to pay their respects.

In addition to hundreds who squeezed into the building, at least two hundred more stood on the grounds, waiting to enter in sections to offer condolences to the Patterson family. The caskets sat end to end at the foot of the stage in the auditorium with American flags draped over them.

The back wall and the sides of the stage were covered with flowers. An honor guard from the Jesse C. Rains American Legion Post 209 stood ramrod straight behind the caskets during the entire two-hour ceremony.

"I can still see those two caskets there," Lamar resident Hannah Oeltjen said more than seventy-five years after she crossed the Memorial Hall stage. "It was the first time I had ever seen a corpse," she said. "It was kind of scary for a five-year-old."

In mid-July 1945, one of the three men involved in the robbery and murders, Victor Monroe Rush, twenty-four, was arrested in Dallas, Texas, where he was living with his wife and three children. The killers' leader, George Sylvester Huston, thirty-seven, was arrested on July 29, 1945, at a Kansas City pool hall.

Huston had a lengthy criminal record dating back to 1918, when he was placed in an Iowa reform facility at age eleven. He had spent several years in the Illinois state penitentiary in Joliet after being convicted of forgery.

The third suspect, George Huston's younger brother Ernest, was captured in early August. When Ernest Huston was returned to Lamar, he told officers how the murders occurred. As he was confessing, an angry mob began to gather, similar to what had happened twenty-six years earlier. Huston was taken out a back door and transported to a jail in a neighboring county.

While they awaited trial, Ernest Huston and Monroe Rush were held in the Greene County Jail in Springfield; George Huston was in the Newton County Jail in Neosho.

Fearful of a recurrence of the 1919 lynching of Jay Lynch, the preliminary hearing for the Huston brothers was held three days earlier than what was written on the court docket.

Highway patrol troopers were able to sneak them into the Barton County Courthouse without the public's knowledge. The judge, Barton County Prosecuting Attorney Roth Faubion, Special Prosecutor Lynn Ewing from Nevada and the lawyers were the only ones there as the suspects waived their preliminary hearings and were then spirited out of the courtroom and returned to jail.

The hearing for Monroe Rush was delayed, but word spread that Rush had confessed to being the one who killed the Pattersons and said he had fired all of the shots except one, which was fired by Sheriff Patterson.

On October 23, 1945, Rush and the Huston brothers pleaded guilty to first-degree murder and were sentenced to life in prison.

The Huston brothers, who served their sentence at the state penitentiary in Jefferson City, had one brief shot at freedom in November 1948, when they were given permission to attend their mother's funeral.

The highway patrol troopers who escorted them allowed the Hustons to go into their mother's house to meet with relatives and friends, one of whom told the troopers a few minutes later that the brothers had slipped out through a back door.

The men were captured within eight days. Ernest Huston was arrested in Richmond, Missouri, at the home of Myrtle Rush, Monroe's mother. His plan was for her to hide him. Instead, she called the police. George Huston was discovered in a barn eighteen miles northeast of Richmond, wrapped in a blanket under a pile of hay.

TRUMAN RETURNS TO LAMAR

*H*arry Truman's first visit to Lamar after leaving as an infant in 1885 took place by accident in 1924. Truman, who was serving his first and only term as Jackson County Court Eastern District judge, had not planned to come to Lamar. The visit was necessitated during a trip to Joplin to attend a convention at the Connor Hotel.

About forty miles from Joplin, Truman hit a pothole and damaged his car. He took a detour and had the damage repaired at a shop in Lamar. When he arrived in Joplin, he penned a letter that evening to Bess, his wife of five years.

In the letter, Truman devoted more words to the pothole that damaged his car and to the convention than he did to his first visit to his hometown. His references to Lamar were limited to two sentences. "We had to make a detour and I went through Lamar, the first time I've been there since I was a year old. I couldn't see much change in the town except that Pop's old livery stable apparently is a garage now."

It was another ten years before Truman returned to the city of his birth, this time as a candidate for U.S. Senate. After serving one term as Jackson County Eastern District judge, he was defeated for reelection in 1926, but with the help of the Pendergast political machine, he returned to office two years later and served two four-year terms as Jackson County Court presiding judge and then launched his bid for the Senate, bringing his campaign to Lamar on May 25, 1934.

In that day's *Lamar Democrat*, Arthur Aull described Truman as an "eminent Kansas City contender for the U.S. Senate seat" and noted that he was "the son of the late John Truman who was in the horse and mule business in Lamar." Aull lavished the candidate with praise. "He is a man that as the ordinary folks come to know him they will like and respect. He likes to meet people, he has a level head and a straightforward way of putting things."

Aull brushed aside critics who said Truman would be following the bidding of political boss Tom Pendergast. "Truman would use his own head in the Senate. Pendergast wouldn't even try to contact him."

Truman returned to Lamar on July 31, 1934, during the last week before the primary, making a brief midmorning speech at the bandstand on the Barton County Courthouse lawn, in which he attempted to appeal to rural voters by telling them of his own background in agriculture, managing the 640-acre Truman farm. He said he could relate to their problems.

Following his speech, Truman walked around the square, shaking hands and meeting as many potential voters as possible.

Truman won the primary and general elections and, after serving six years in the Senate, returned to Lamar during his 1940 reelection campaign. This time, Truman was the underdog, as Pendergast was sitting in a federal prison and two of the men responsible for putting him there, Governor Lloyd Stark and Jackson County prosecuting attorney Maurice Milligan, were Truman's opponents in the Democratic primary.

Both men attempted to link Truman with the corruption that put Pendergast behind bars, and they received help from Arthur Aull, who threw his full support behind Stark.

Truman campaigned in Lamar on July 29, 1940, speaking in front of the bandstand on the Barton County Courthouse lawn. In his coverage in the *Democrat*, Aull did not make a single reference to Truman being a Lamar native.

One of Truman's primary opponents, Maurice Milligan, spoke in Lamar the following day. Aull praised the speech in the July 30 *Democrat* but wrote that Lamar and Barton County residents should vote for Stark and not let Milligan split the vote.

The overwhelming majority of Democrats, because his victory would mark a great victory for the Pendergast machine, are against nominating Senator Truman. Since they feel that way and there is no doubt that they do, even though they might prefer Honorable Maurice Milligan to Gov. Stark, they must admit that the facts which confront them prove their one way to leave no doubt about the defeat of Sen. Truman is to cast their ballots for Gov. Stark.

Aull by concluded by writing, "Let us all unite in this fight to give the old machine the knockout blow."

Barton County followed Aull's advice the following Tuesday, delivering 1,386 votes to Stark, 514 for Truman and 315 for Milligan. Surrounding counties voted for Truman, giving an indication of how much influence Aull had.

Statewide, Stark and Milligan combined for more votes than Truman, splitting the vote and providing Truman with an eight-thousand-vote victory. In November, Truman won reelection with 51 percent of the vote.

TRUMAN, NATIONAL MEDIA
COME TO LAMAR

*T*he circumstances behind Harry S. Truman's first visit to Lamar since the 1940 Senate primary campaign, and his most important visit, were somewhat unusual.

It was after Truman received the vice-presidential nomination at the Democratic National Convention in Chicago on July 24, 1944, that two leading citizens saw an opportunity to promote Lamar.

Almost immediately after the convention, while drinking coffee in the Travelers Hotel dining room with owner H.C. Chancellor, Mayor Guy Ross and Lamar Chamber of Commerce president Raymond River, both Republicans, devised the idea of inviting Democratic vice-presidential nominee Truman to return to Lamar and open his campaign.

Since Ross had met Truman once—though they were by no means friends—he was the one who wrote the message. The following telegram was sent to Truman at the Stevens Hotel in Chicago: "The people of Lamar, regardless of party, are proud of you and invite you to open your campaign in the city of your birth."

The telegram was signed by Guy Ross, mayor; Raymond River, president of the Chamber of Commerce; William S. Lowery, commander of the Jesse C. Rains Post 209; and R.F. Ryder, commander of the Yowell Frow Post 3691.

Despite the enthusiasm of Ross and River, the general consensus was that, while the invitation was worth a try, the chances were almost nonexistent that Truman would open his campaign in Lamar, a town he left when he was ten months old and had visited sparingly since.

On August 8, National Democratic Party chairman Robert Hannegan announced that Truman would probably come to Lamar on August 29 and that President Roosevelt would make the final decision.

Roosevelt's decision was revealed to Truman during a meeting on August 18 at the White House, which Truman described in a letter to Bess, who was in Independence:

> *I told the President that you were in Missouri attending to my business there and he said that was OK. He gave me a lot of hooey about what I could do to help the campaign and said he thought I ought to go home for an official notification and then go to Detroit for a labor speech and make no more engagements until we had had another conference.*
>
> *So that's what I am going to do.*

Even with the date for Truman's Lamar campaign stop changed from Tuesday, August 29, to Thursday, August 31, city officials had less than two weeks to prepare. Though it was unlikely any of them realized it, Truman's speech in Lamar would end up being one of the most important in the 1944 presidential campaign and in Truman's political career.

More than two hundred attended a hastily scheduled planning meeting at Memorial Hall conducted by River, Ross and the other executive committee members, Rubey Ryder and William Lowery.

Options for a location for the speech were debated. Though the city park and Lamar High School football field were considered, the decision was made to hold the event on the west side of the Barton County Courthouse, with speakers standing on a special platform that would be built over the steps.

Since a city of three thousand did not have enough hotel rooms or dining facilities to handle the number of radio, newspaper and wire service reporters, as well as national and regional Democratic political officials who planned to be at the ceremony, many of the events would have to be held in Joplin, forty miles from Lamar. That concerned Lamar officials and Aull, who suspected Joplin would steal the event.

Joplin Chamber of Commerce president George A. Spiva, dealing both with Republicans who were critical of the city's involvement in a Democratic Party campaign event and Lamar officials' suspicions, said it was simply the chamber's way to help "a neighbor from the north."

River made the city's position clear in a phone call to Democratic National Committee secretary Bill Boyle, in which the *Democrat* reported he said, "You want to have the affair at Joplin, bring Truman up, have a few minutes, put on a brief ceremony and leave for Joplin again. If you are going to do that, just hold your darned meeting on some street corner in Joplin."

Cooler heads prevailed, and it appeared that the Truman visit was set, until the day before, when a torrential downpour, more than an inch and a half of rain, hit Lamar. Truman arrived at the Connor Hotel in Joplin that day; an informal dinner was held in the evening and a breakfast the following morning.

After the breakfast, Truman took a motorcade twenty miles south of Joplin to visit troops at Camp Crowder just outside of Neosho at the invitation of Post Commandant General Walter Prosser. Along with Truman, the motorcade included a contingent of twenty-four of his Democratic colleagues from the Senate; Joplin Chamber of Commerce president Spiva; Jasper County Democratic chairman Paul Van Pool; and Harry Easley of Webb City, who was serving as state coordinator for the Truman visit,

Camp Crowder was one of many bases constructed during the buildup to war in 1941. Truman's visit occurred on the third anniversary of the ground-breaking for the camp on August 30, 1941.

The camp, initially intended as a site to train infantry, served primarily as the largest training center in the country for the U.S. Army Signal Corps, but it served other purposes, including housing German and Italian prisoners of war.

Truman was shown a large portion of the camp, though it was impossible to see even half of it, as Camp Crowder covered forty-three thousand acres. After sharing a meal with the soldiers, Truman and his entourage left the camp to begin the sixty-mile trek to Lamar.

The stormy weather that had dumped an inch and a half of rain on Lamar the previous day disappeared. Not only did it appear the rain would not return on Truman Day, but there also wasn't a cloud in the sky. The square was roped off; no traffic was allowed except delivery trucks. Sandwich stands were set up just off the square on each corner, while churches served as dining halls for the throngs of visitors. With wartime gasoline rationing in place, rides were shared from nearby communities and by some attending from hundreds of miles away.

The thirty-by-fifty-foot platform where Truman would speak was in place at the west steps of the Barton County Courthouse. Banners were hung around the square. The National Democratic Committee paid for $1,500 worth of decorations. The railway stations were also decorated so that anyone arriving for the speech would know they were attending a political event.

The Palace Drug Store was turned into the headquarters for state, regional and national press, with Aull and his daughter Madeleine Aull Van Hafften serving as hosts.

The wives and daughters of visiting dignitaries were greeted at the Travelers Hotel by a welcoming committee consisting of Goldia Ross, Mayor Guy Ross's wife; Pearl Chancellor; Luanna Aull; Mrs. Ed Stephens; and Ila Gathman, wife of City Councilman Loyd Gathman. Harry Truman's wife, Bess, and their daughter, Margaret, were among those welcomed by the committee.

In the biography that Margaret Truman wrote about her father in 1972, she made clear her disdain for spending August 31, 1944, in Lamar. "It was a day to remember—or forget—depending on your point of view. One thing was certain. It [the notification ceremony] was too big for Lamar. Toilet facilities and the sewage system broke down. The parking field was turned into a huge mud hole by a heavy rainstorm the previous day. Poor Harry Easley, who was the chairman in charge of the day, almost went crazy."

Politicians were not the only visitors to Lamar on Truman Day. At least four people were victims of pickpockets—and those were just the ones Aull found out about and dutifully reported in the pages of the *Democrat*.

In addition to pickpockets, Lamar found itself besieged by what Aull described as "smooth looking operators, teams of 'crapshooters' that were preying on men who let their guards down with just a bit of encouragement. They enticed their victims into games with a drink." And there were plenty of drinks available in Lamar that day. Mayor Guy Ross reported that twenty thousand bottles of beer had been shipped to the city's three taverns.

Truman and the traveling party of national and state officials arrived in Lamar two hours later than expected, greeted by a performance from the Lamar High School Band. The streets were lined with signs of support for the Roosevelt-Truman ticket and banners proclaiming, "Welcome Home, Harry." Seven marching bands, including bands from Springfield, Joplin and Carthage, in addition to the Lamar High School Band, played patriotic tunes.

Mayor Ross and the welcoming committee greeted Truman and the visitors. Following a parade and a concert featuring local and visiting bands, an informal reception was held at the Travelers Hotel, followed by a banquet at 5:00 p.m. at Memorial Hall. Another band concert entertained the people who gathered on the Lamar Square at 7:00 p.m. as thousands waited to hear from the vice-presidential candidate.

Truman was not the only person returning to Lamar. Arriving late that afternoon to hear her son give his speech was his ninety-two-year-old mother, Martha Ellen Young Truman, who had recently broken her hip.

Major General Ralph Truman, Harry Truman's cousin, drove Mattie Truman and her daughter Mary Jane, who lived with her in Independence, into the city. It had been arranged for the car to be allowed onto the square, and an area had been set aside directly by the speakers' platform so that Mrs. Truman, who was almost completely blind, could hear her son speak.

The Truman speech, which would have been well covered, especially by the regional and state media, became a national event for a number of reasons. With President Roosevelt managing the war (and with his health failing in the final year of his life), Truman's speech would be the first Democratic event of the presidential campaign.

When Truman accepted the vice-presidential nomination in Chicago, he spoke only a few words. Democratic Party officials noted that the Republicans had been provided a half hour of national network coverage when their vice-presidential candidate, Ohio governor John Bricker, spoke at the GOP convention. They demanded equal time.

J. Leonard Reinsch, who scheduled radio time for the national ticket, dealt with network officials, who felt they had complied with equal-time requirements when they broadcast Truman's brief thank-you. If Truman wanted the airtime, they contended, he should have talked longer. Reinsch was finally able to convince the networks to broadcast the Lamar speech live.

That made Truman's Lamar speech not only his first campaign event but also his vice-presidential nomination acceptance speech.

Reinsch was responsible for making sure the candidate was ready for prime time. Truman, not known as an orator, spoke much too fast.

"Obviously, the first problem was to slow the candidate down in his delivery, and second, to bring more emphasis to the important points and make a better radio presentation than is normally the case with someone with the Midwestern twang, or a Missouri twang, whatever you want to call it," Reinsch remembered. Truman still kept rushing through his practice sessions until Reinsch devised a plan.

"I started the idea of putting less and less material on each page, so he would have to turn pages frequently. The turning of the pages would take time and the mechanical process would slow down his delivery."

"The Lamar speech was a real headache," Reinsch said, not only describing Truman but also the man who was scheduled to introduce him, Senator Tom Connally of Texas. In his deals with the networks, Reinsch only received thirty minutes of broadcast time, but the stem-winding Connally, known for his soaring oratory, had a much longer speech than Reinsch preferred.

After discussing the situation with Connally, the speech was reworked to about ten minutes, but after Truman's team thought the revisions had been completed, Connally began adding material. Reinsch feared that Connally would keep the networks from being able to broadcast all of Truman's speech.

These things were a concern for Democratic Party officials, but for Lamar residents, Truman Day was a break from bad news and tragic events that had plagued the area during a time when many of its young men were fighting overseas.

Two weeks earlier, three men had murdered Barton County sheriff Roy Patterson and his son Sammie. On Truman Day, those men were still at large. Earlier that month, Travelers Hotel owner H.C. Chancellor had received a letter from the War Department informing him that his son Richard was missing in action. Other parents had received the same message about their sons.

Less than three weeks earlier, on August 12, a page-one article in the *Lamar Democrat* broke the news that a young Lamar man, Donald Quillin, son of Mr. and Mrs. Charley Quillin, had been killed in France. Quillin, twenty-five, was a member of the Lamar High School class of 1938. "The loss of this gallant and young Lamar boy has brought the war and its tragedy ever closer to Lamar," Aull wrote.

Truman Day was a break from the grim reality that had enveloped Lamar residents, and they were eagerly anticipating the vice-presidential nominee's return to his hometown.

The style of dress was anything but casual. The men were dressed in their Sunday best, though in a nod to the August heat, they dispensed with jackets. The women were not only wearing their finest dresses but were also sporting new hats, many purchased during the various Truman Day sales.

The crowd moved as close as it could to the newly constructed speakers' platform, which featured gigantic photos of President Roosevelt and Truman. The introduction was given by Mayor Guy Ross, who then introduced Sam Weir, the Democratic state chairman. Reverend Cecil Lasley gave the invocation.

The next portion of the program featured the introduction of dignitaries, including state officials and a host of Truman's fellow senators: Tom Connally of Texas, Joseph Guffey of Pennsylvania, Carl A. Hatch of New Mexico, John L. McClellan of Arkansas, Ernest W. McFarland of Arizona, Elmer Thomas of Oklahoma, Claude Pepper of Florida and D.W. Clark of Idaho.

National radio coverage began with Connally's notification address. After his speech, Truman stepped onto the platform, drawing heavy applause.

Truman opened with a formal acknowledgement of the purpose of his appearance and said it would be a mistake to change the commander in chief when the nation was at war. There was no one who could steer this country to victory any better than Franklin D. Roosevelt. He praised the efforts of U.S. soldiers and sailors and said those efforts and Roosevelt's leadership put the Allies on the brink of winning the war, but the victory still must be won.

"Military victory over Germany is but a step," Truman said, noting that the United States then had to triumph over Japan and then prepare for the new world that would emerge from those victories.

Another reason to keep Roosevelt in the White House, Truman said, was the amount of time it would take for a new president to get up to speed.

> *It takes time for anyone to familiarize himself with a new job. That is particularly true of the President of the United States, the most difficult and complex job in the world. Even in peacetime, it is well recognized that it takes a new president at least a year to learn the fundamentals of the job.*
>
> *We cannot expect any man wholly inexperienced in national and international affairs to readily learn the views, the objectives and the inner thoughts of such divergent personalities as those dominant leaders who have guided the destinies of our courageous allies. There will be no time to learn, and once mistakes are made, they cannot be unmade.*

Ironically, Truman himself would be placed in such a position eight months later.

After Truman's speech, his mother told a reporter she had not minded the long trip to Lamar. "I think it would have been worth coming from California to hear. There isn't a finer man living than Harry Truman."

The visit was her last to the city where she had given birth to the future president.

MADELEINE AULL VAN HAFFTEN

W hen Truman was sworn in as vice president on Saturday, January 20, 1945, he was not the only one who received increased scrutiny from national newspapers and magazines. Attention was also turned toward the city where he was born.

The most popular publication of that era, Henry Luce's *Life* magazine, featured a profile of *Lamar Democrat* publisher Arthur Aull titled "Aull Prints All the News."

Aull, seventy-two, had received national attention through the writing of Hearst columnist Ted Cook, but even Hearst did not have the readership of *Life*, which was estimated at thirteen million.

On page eight of the February 26, 1945 edition, writer John R. Cauley explained the essence of Aull's brand of small-town reporting.

> *Arthur Aull, editor and owner of the Lamar, MO Democrat for 44 years, operated on the simple theory that the function of a newspaper is to print all the news. Unlike most country editors whose papers reflect their own native caution and orthodoxy, Editor Aull believes it is his duty to tell literally everything that happens in his town. So far, Mr. Aull has been sued three times, unsuccessfully, and assaulted only once.*

Cauley provided several samples of Aull's reporting and described how Aull did not subscribe to wire services but wrote the contents of the *Democrat* each day himself, except for the women's news and club news, which his wife, Luanna, wrote.

The *Life* article provided a complete news story Aull had written about the kind of event that would never make it into the pages of any other newspaper in the nation. In it, Aull wrote about the birth of a son to a bookkeeper at a Lamar bank and how the bank's cashier married her at her hospital bedside. Aull emphasized that the woman was unaware she was pregnant and that no one in the bank suspected, including the father of the child.

Aull noted that the cashier was fifty-three and his bride only thirty-three and that "None of the folks at the bank where (she) worked day after day suspected. There apparently wasn't a whisper from the sharp-eyed gossips."

Aull concluded the report with his assessment of what happened. "Well, true enough, there never was a better girl than (she) and we all know (he) is a grand old boy, but God, it was badly managed."

Aull told Cauley his purpose was to set the record straight and stop lies from spreading through gossip.

With the death of President Roosevelt on April 12, 1945, Harry S. Truman became commander in chief. While the news media descended upon his hometown of Independence, Lamar also received more attention, including another *Life* profile, and the *Lamar Democrat* benefited from that attention.

By this time, however, Aull was beginning to turn over more of his responsibilities to Madeleine Aull Van Hafften, the oldest of his three daughters. While Aull's other daughters, Betty and Genevieve, attended the University of Missouri School of Journalism, Madeleine, the daughter who eventually succeeded Aull, did not, and that did not bother him at all. She attended the University of Missouri but did not enter journalism school. After graduating, she was a teacher for several years in Kansas City schools.

"When I went away to Missouri University and told him I was going to major in journalism, he blew his top," she recalled. "He said, 'You'll do nothing of the sort! You'll take arts and sciences and learn things you need to know.' My father told me I was the one who should take over the newspaper because he wouldn't have to pound journalism schooling out of my head like he would have had to do with my sisters."

Madeleine received a firsthand example of her father's dedication to the newspaper after a disgruntled reader attacked him. The story was picked up by the Associated Press on August 12, 1943. "Arthur Aull, veteran publisher of the *Lamar Democrat*, was nursing a cut and a bruised head today, the result of an encounter with two irate women readers, one of whom wielded a club." The woman, upset by an article in which Aull wrote about what she considered to be her private life, struck him on the head eight to ten times.

Lamar Democrat editor Madeleine Aull Van Hafften is shown seated at her desk. Nell Casement, who worked for the newspaper for thirty years, is standing behind her. © Springfield News-Leader, USA TODAY *Network*.

Aull took a taxi home, and a doctor was summoned to treat the wounds. While waiting for the doctor, though still bleeding, Aull recognized a good story and dictated the details of his beating to Madeleine, including a cheery conclusion: "Fortunately, we wore our old straw hat, which was some protection, and we have a rather heavy head of hair which protected us some. It would certainly have ruined a bald-headed guy with no hat."

Eventually, Aull's illnesses left him confined to his home, and on May 7, 1948, one week after he suffered a massive heart attack, Madeleine wrote her father's obituary, which began, "Arthur Aull, 75, nationally known, widely quoted editor of this paper and father of the writer, is dead." Her article ran seventy column inches, detailed his career and described Aull as a "great patriot and civic leader" who was "devoted to the Democratic Party."

Aull's funeral was held on Monday, May 10, at Memorial Hall. All businesses were closed at the request of Lamar mayor Carol Combs, and more than five hundred people came to pay their respects to a man who had played a prominent role in their lives for nearly a half century.

Aull's friend Judge John Flanigan from Carthage delivered the eulogy, which included a reading of Aull's "Creed of Life," which he had published in the *Democrat* in 1921; poetry; and his tribute to the deceased. "The death of Arthur Aull has cost Lamar its foremost citizen. Journalism has lost one of its brightest stars and truth has lost a loyal friend."

Aull's widow, Luanna, and her three daughters received condolences from across the nation, including a telegram from President Truman's press secretary, Charles G. Ross. "The president was greatly distressed to hear of the death of Mr. Arthur Aull, widely known editor of the *Lamar Democrat*. An able and picturesque figure in American journalism has passed on."

After her father's death, Madeleine was determined to run the *Democrat* just as her father had done for nearly half a century. She followed the same rounds across the city every morning as her father had done for decades and spared no details, no matter how grim, gruesome or embarrassing, of anything that happened in Lamar.

Madeleine, however, ran headlong into the prejudices of the time. Women at small-town newspapers in the 1940s were supposed to write social news and print recipes. Arthur Aull not only had the advantage of being the right gender for the time; he also had a distinguished scholarly look that commanded respect.

Along with the rampant sexism of the time, Madeleine was often judged by her appearance. Her wardrobe invariably consisted of long, dark-colored dresses, and her hair was pulled up severely in a bun and was normally covered by one of her collection of colorful hats.

When people entered the *Democrat* office on the north side of the square, Madeleine's desk was one of the first things they saw. They were also greeted by the slight haze caused by Madeleine's chain-smoking.

Madeleine was not the stern presence at the *Democrat* that her outward appearance or her writing may have indicated. Though her language could sometimes be rough, she was not feared among her coworkers.

"I had the greatest respect for Madeleine," said Dorothy Parks, who was a typesetter. "People always made fun of her, this weird little woman with the hat on and she always had a serious look on her face, but she always worked hard. She headed out the door in the morning with a pad and pencil and she would come back in about 11 a.m. and start writing and by three or four o'clock she would have everything back to us."

Madeleine continued to follow her father's teachings without any variance. Where Aull never hesitated to call a scoundrel a scoundrel, neither did his daughter. Both, however, had one type of person who was never to be criticized.

"I went in one day when she was typing up someone's obituary. She was just moaning and groaning," Parks recalled. "I said, 'Madeleine, what's wrong? What's the matter?'

"'Well, Dorothy, my dad always told me you can't call a dead man a son of a bitch.' She wanted to call him an SOB, but she couldn't do it. She had to find some nicer things to write about him."

Madeleine also lacked her father's business acumen, and when the *Democrat* faced a severe challenge from a competitor, the *Lamar Journal*, in the 1950s, it came close to going out of business. Another member of the Aull family came to the rescue.

Luanna Aull, who had replaced her husband as publisher while Madeleine handled the editorial duties, announced in the September 29, 1953 *Democrat* that her son-in-law Stanley White was the newspaper's new business manager. Though it was not spelled out, White, who was married to the Aulls' youngest daughter, Betty, would essentially handle the publishing duties.

Though White's background was primarily in radio, he had successfully rescued another newspaper that had run into financial problems when he served as advertising manager in Hope, Arkansas, which in 1993 became better known as the hometown of another president, Bill Clinton.

After Stan and Betty White arrived in Lamar, the *Democrat* truly became a family newspaper, with Madeleine continuing to handle the news, Betty writing social items and Stan selling advertising and writing sports. With the addition of the Whites to the newspaper, the *Democrat*'s financial picture improved immediately.

Ten months after the Whites arrived, the competition ended when the *Democrat* bought the *Journal* and shut it down.

Newspapers moved from hot type to offset printing, leaving the *Lamar Democrat* looking like a relic of the past. Other changes also did not sit well with Madeleine, and she let *Democrat* readers know. She had no use for women's liberation, the changes in her beloved Democratic Party or the civil rights movement.

After President John F. Kennedy's June 11, 1963 speech announcing that he would seek landmark civil rights legislation, Madeleine forcefully expressed her opposition. "Two wrongs don't make a right," she wrote in the June 25 edition. "We are constantly reminded of this as we observe the President and his Negro advisers urge that Congress pass legislation accelerating treatment preferential to the negro over other voices."

Madeleine acknowledged that it was wrong to deprive African Americans of the vote, but added, "There were good reasons for it in the post–Civil War period."

She added that hotel and swimming pool owners "should not have to open their facilities to negroes."

She felt the same disdain for the women's rights movement. "I've never been a bit sympathetic to the movement," she was quoted in her obituary in the November 22, 1977 *Springfield Leader and Press*. "I've always felt I've been on equal footing with a man. Any woman who has the ability and know-how can get what she wants if she is willing to work at it."

The Aull era at the *Democrat* finally came to an end in 1972, when the family sold the newspaper to Missouri secretary of state James Kirkpatrick. Luanna died in 1968 at age ninety-five, and there were no younger family members to continue the tradition.

Madeleine had divorced Carl Van Hafften more than twenty years earlier, following the Aull tradition of telling the entire story on page one of the newspaper. The couple had no children, and Madeleine was seventy-four. Stan and Betty White also had no children. Neither Genevieve Turrentine, Arthur Aull's third daughter, nor her children had any desire to run the *Democrat*.

Despite that, they had not planned to sell the newspaper until they were approached by Kirkpatrick, who, in addition to being a politician, was in the newspaper business, having served as editor at the *Warrensburg Daily Star-Journal* and the *Jefferson City News Tribune* and later owning the *Windsor Review*.

After the sale, Madeleine lived quietly at the same house at 400 West Eleventh Street where she had lived with Arthur and Luanna Aull for the previous thirty-five years, just a few blocks from the square and the *Democrat*. "I don't remember Madeleine ever coming back to the *Democrat* office," Dorothy Parks said.

"I have been at loose ends since the sale," Madeleine told a *St. Louis Post-Dispatch* reporter six weeks after the sale. "It was a traumatic experience. One of my difficulties will be keeping myself occupied." She said she planned to write, but the words she wrote in her farewell article in the *Democrat* were the last she shared with readers.

The final reminder of the Aull brand of journalism came in the November 22, 1977 *Springfield News-Leader*, in which she described her philosophy. "My father gave me two pieces of advice. Tell everything and tell it just as if you were talking. Sometimes certain people were not pleased about the tell everything part. I believe a newspaper should be a mirror of the community in that it reflects exactly what goes on in the community, good or bad. No newspaper is going to have the confidence of a community if it plays favorites."

Madeleine Aull Van Hafften died on November 21, 1977, one day after her seventy-ninth birthday. Her words were included in her obituary.

BROTHER ADAMS AND HIS MULES

Though Lamar was not a part of the 1948 presidential campaign in which Harry Truman unexpectedly was elected to a full term, the city played a role in Truman's inauguration.

It was decided that Lamar, where Truman was born in 1884, the son of a simple mule trader and his wife, would be represented by a wagon drawn by a team of Missouri mules. Two of the mules were owned by Claude "Brother" Adams, who raised mules at the southeast corner of the intersection of Highways 160 and 71 just west of Lamar. The other two were owned by Ed Knell of Carthage.

Adams, forty-three, who had been raising mules since 1914, when he was nine, was proud of his mules. Word of Lamar's representation in the inaugural parade spread quickly due to coverage from regional newspapers and wire services and locally through the *Democrat*. "Every one of my mules has won a blue ribbon somewhere,' Adams told a United Press reporter. "They're fine mules. We like to think we're breeding as good a mule as you'll find anywhere in Missouri."

The animals Adams and Knell were taking to Washington, D.C., were created by breeding the jacks with Belgian mares. The four sleek, 1,200-pound blond sorrel mules—Blondie and Duke, owned by Adams, and Beck, and Polly, owned by Knell—were distinguished by their flowing white manes, tails and undersides.

Though initially there was talk of taking the mules to Washington by train, those plans fell through, and Blondie, Duke, Beck and Polly were loaded into a stock truck.

Brother's brother Billee Bob Adams was in charge of getting the contingent—himself; Knell; Brother; Brother's wife, Hazel; and their five-year-old son, Claude Oscar—to the nation's capital.

B.B., twenty-eight, began driving a truck at age fourteen, working with Brother and hauling coal from the coal veins in the small Barton County community of Milford. After serving in the U.S. Navy during the war, Adams bought two trucks and a combine and, accompanied by Hazel and daughters Tina and Frances, followed the wheat harvest through several states before returning to Lamar in 1947, where he operated a trucking business.

The inaugural parade lasted three hours, with General Omar Bradley, chief of staff of the army, serving as grand marshal. Cadets from West Point, Annapolis and the Coast Guard Academy represented the armed forces in the parade, while each state had bands and marching units.

The appearance of Brother Adams's and Ed Knell's sorrel mules was one of the highlights of the parade. Adams and Knell, dressed in white overalls, drove the team down Pennsylvania Avenue hitched to a light spring rubber-tired wagon with the words "Lamar, Missouri, the birthplace of President Harry S. Truman" written in bold, prominent letters on the side.

Brother Adams offered the highest praise he could give a president to Harry Truman in a United Press interview. "He seems to know a lot about mules."

Adams's opinion of Truman's knowledge was confirmed on October 16, 1963, at the annual American Royal Livestock and Horse Show in Kansas City. To the delight of the crowd of 6,500, the judge for the show, Harry S. Truman, entered the arena in a wagon drawn by four sorrel mules. Truman told reporters that evening, "The best mules I ever drove were six gray mules that belonged to my uncle. I remember the lead pair were named Pearl and Fanny."

The first-place winner among the nine mules entered in the competition was a two-year-old named Jane, owned by Brother Adams of Lamar, whose mules had made such a fine showing in the inaugural parade fourteen years earlier.

TRUMAN'S LAST VISIT TO LAMAR

While Harry S. Truman made no visits to Lamar in the first few years after he left the White House in January 1953, the former president still made news in the city where he was born.

In 1953, for the first time, Lamar residents were able to dial for long-distance calls, instead of having calls placed by an operator. Loyd Gathman, serving his first year as mayor after more than a decade on the city council, was given the honor of making the first call. That call went to Truman.

"I apologized to him for calling," Gathman recalled, "and we had an ordinary conversation. He said it was nice of me to call and he was very grateful."

When *Lamar Journal* reporter Marvin Van Gilder was attempting to establish the Barton County Historical Society that same year, he wrote Truman, who responded with a supportive message:

> *In reply to yours of July 23, I think it is a grand thing for you to organize a Barton County Historical Society. It will be a wonderful thing for you to work in cooperation with the State Historical Society and I know you can make a contribution that will be well worthwhile.*
>
> *I was born in Lamar on May 8, 1884, but left there for Cass and Jackson counties when I was about a year old and was not able to get back to Lamar again until the senatorial campaign of 1934. I have always thought very highly of Lamar.*
>
> *Sincerely yours,*
> *Harry S Truman*

Truman did not return to Lamar until the end of the decade. After the UAW paid $6,000 in 1957 for the house where Truman was born, the next two years were spent restoring the home to the way it would have been on May 8, 1884. When the project was completed, a dedication was scheduled for April 19, 1959.

Gathman was determined that Lamar put its best foot forward when Truman and the national media returned to the city for the dedication. It was not the first time Gathman had been involved with the planning for a Truman visit. He was serving on the city council on August 31, 1944, when Truman accepted the vice-presidential nomination.

Gathman issued a notice encouraging city residents to make sure their lawns were "neatly clipped and flowers displayed if possible." Arranging the dedication ceremony took a great deal of diplomacy on Gathman's part, as he recalled in a 1984 interview. "The United Auto Workers felt they should have their say and I agreed. The state had some ideas." As Gathman worked to satisfy both sides, some of the plans city officials had for the dedication were discarded. "A lot of our ideas were bypassed," he said.

During the week before the April 19 dedication, city workers poured gravel on the unpaved edges of blacktopped streets and swept the side streets alongside the street where the home was located, which as a result of council action had been rechristened Truman Street.

American flags were placed on light poles, and signs welcoming Truman were placed prominently throughout the route he would be taking and where visitors would be able to see them.

A welcoming committee was appointed to greet the former president when he arrived. Mayor Gathman and Bud Moore arranged a speakers' stand for the dedication ceremony, with Lamar School District superintendent Ted Windes arranging for the school's public address system to be moved to the birthplace.

The *Lamar Democrat* office was set up as a media center, with Luanna Aull, Madeleine Aull Van Hafften and Stan and Betty White serving as hosts. Though there would be no live national radio or television broadcasts, network reporters were there, as once again were representatives of the wire services and the *New York Times*.

Reporters from the Kansas City, St. Louis and Springfield newspapers crowded into the *Democrat* office, as well as their counterparts with the *Joplin Globe* and *Joplin News-Herald*.

City officials were concerned about the weather when it rained the previous evening, and the skies were still cloudy on the morning of April 19. But the sky was clear by the time the former president arrived.

The long day for Harry Truman, who was now less than a month from his seventy-fifth birthday, began that morning in Independence, when approximately one thousand people gathered on the square to watch as seven covered wagons drawn by horses and Missouri mules departed the city on a trip to Oregon.

Wagon master Gordon "Tex" Serpa was leading a caravan of twenty-one Oregon residents—a dozen men, six women and three children—all dressed in 1840s clothing on the two-thousand-mile trek from Independence, Missouri, to Independence, Oregon, as part of Oregon's centennial celebration. The trip was officially known as the "On to Oregon Cavalcade."

A few moments before the long journey began, Serpa and those who were with him in the lead wagon talked with Truman, who was serving as honorary wagon master. The former president wished them well, and as the barricade was lifted so the wagons could leave, Truman called out, "Westward ho! God bless you! Let her go!"

After the wagons left and the crowd dissipated, Truman was on his way to the dedication. Originally, Bess had been scheduled to make the trip with him, but she was not feeling well and decided to remain in Independence.

In those years before former presidents were automatically provided Secret Service protection, there was no protection for Truman, and there was also no chauffeur or limousine to take the president the 125 miles to Lamar. Truman drove from Independence to Lamar, arriving in the city at 11:30 a.m., earlier than expected, surprising the welcoming committee and various state officials and dignitaries at the Travelers Hotel.

From the Travelers, Truman made his first visit to the house where he was born since 1944. Joseph Jaeger Jr., the state parks director, showed Truman the improvements that had been made. Truman expressed his approval, adding, "It looks a little different than I remember it."

In one bedroom, two photos on the wall captured Truman's attention. One was of him as a baby, and the other was of Martha Truman. Truman's next stop was the home of an old friend, Harriet Spradling, for a private buffet luncheon in the dining room and on the patio.

From 1:00 p.m. to 3:30 p.m., a reception honoring Truman's old army unit, Battery D, was held at Memorial Hall. As the reception neared its conclusion, the crowd, later estimated at around seven thousand, began to gather at the Truman home in anticipation of the dedication ceremony.

Shortly after 3:30 p.m., a parade led by the Lamar High School Band and the Thirty-Fifth Division, Missouri National Guard Band, started at the square and made the four-block trek to the Truman house. Truman, whose morning routine in Independence always included a walk through his neighborhood, kept up with the bands' brisk pace as he walked behind them.

Lamar residents and out-of-town visitors stood side-by-side the entire length of the parade route, cheering as Truman passed. The smile never left the former president's face as he waved his hat at the crowds and stopped occasionally to talk to someone, usually a child.

Randall Jessee, director of the Metropolitan Area Planning Council in Kansas City, served as master of ceremonies, introducing UAW vice president Leonard Woodcock, who substituted for President Walter Reuther, who was unable to be in Lamar due to a throat infection.

Woodcock officially presented the deed to the Truman house to Missouri governor James Blair, who promised that the state would "preserve this site as a show place for all the world."

Blair continued: "The men and women of the United Auto Workers, led by their gifted president make this gift because they believe in what President Truman stood for in his public career. We in Missouri accept it with pleasure because President Truman, by his life and works, has become the number one citizen of our state."

A highlight of the ceremony followed as seventeen-year-old Donald Braker, Lamar High School Student Council president, stepped to the microphone to present Truman with a plaque from the people of Lamar.

Braker's dark suit was accentuated by a white carnation on his lapel. If the teenager was nervous, he showed no sign of it. Public speaking was nothing new for Braker. Only two days earlier at the Missouri Future Farmers of America Convention, Braker had captured first place in oratory.

Braker turned to Truman and said, "You are symbolic of every American boy's secret ambition." He held the bronze plaque and noted that it would be displayed prominently in the house in the room where a future president had been born on May 8, 1884, to offer "vivid proof that wealth and pretentious surroundings aren't necessary for greatness."

The teenager read the inscription. "In this room on May 8, 1884, was born President Harry S. Truman whose faith in the youth of this country has been an inspiration to all. In honest and sincere appreciation—The Citizens of Lamar."

Braker concluded by again turning to the former president and saying, "Lamar is proud of you, its native son."

Truman shook hands with Braker, posed for several photos and said, "You'd better look out for that boy because Missouri may have another occupant in the White House someday."

Senator Stuart Symington delivered the dedicatory address. "Starting today, people will come to Lamar from all over the world. They will be making the pilgrimage to learn about the beginnings of this man of Missouri who wrote for himself an imperishable chapter in history. They will see that what went into the making of Harry Truman was America itself."

Symington stressed that Truman's life would be noteworthy even if he had never become president, "because his life and character have been a mirror of America." He detailed Truman's humble beginning and the early obstacles to his success, when he struggled as a small-business owner, and how he rose above those struggles to reach high office. "On April 12, 1945, Harry S. Truman did become president and what he did for the next seven years will be remembered as long as free men walk the earth."

The final speaker was the one whom thousands had waited to see. Truman, still looking dapper in a navy blue suit that remained unwrinkled despite the full schedule he had followed since serving as honorary wagon master for the caravan leaving Independence that morning, looked out over the crowd taking in the scene before he spoke.

Lamar's most famous native son thanked its citizens, the people of the UAW and everyone else who came to the home on Truman Avenue.

"They don't do this for a former president until he's been dead 50 years. I feel like I've been buried and dug up while I'm still alive and I'm glad they've done it to me today. I am overwhelmed by this immense outpouring of Missourians and people from neighboring states. You don't know how I appreciate all this. I'm extremely touched."

When the ceremony concluded, more than two thousand people lined up to tour the house, with the first visitor being the person who had been born in a small bedroom there almost seventy-five years earlier.

The former president of the United States and U.S. senator from the state of Missouri signed his name to the register, "Harry Truman, Independence, Mo. Retired Farmer."

Truman talked with people outside the house for a while before he made a second trip to the Harriet Spradling home, where he rested before the next activities began. The last stop on Truman's itinerary was the Travelers Hotel, where the UAW gave a dinner in his honor with 240 people attending. The Travelers staff provided a meal that consisted of cold sliced turkey, fried chicken, mashed potatoes, gravy, green beans, spring salad, hot rolls, butter, jelly and relishes with a strawberry chiffon pie and coffee for dessert.

The hotel was filled with laughter as Truman thoroughly enjoyed the company of a room filled with friends. After saying his goodbyes, Truman was back in his car and on the way home to Independence.

On Sunday, April 19, 1959, Lamar showed its appreciation for Harry Truman. It was his last visit to the city where he was born.

14
GERALD GILKEY

*T*he political career of the man who became the longest-serving mayor in the history of Missouri began in 1959, less than one week after Truman's final visit to Lamar.

Gerald Gilkey's rise to political prominence in Lamar would have come as a shock to those who remembered him from his earliest visits to the city, which were primarily weekend excursions to the Lamar Square.

In the years before the United States entered World War II, the Lamar Square served as the favored destination for young people of high school age or a few years older.

On Friday and Saturday nights, especially during the summer months, but any time when the weather was decent, groups of young people in cars began the process of cruising the square early in the evening and continued for hours.

The endless driving was curtailed considerably during the years when gasoline was rationed to support the war effort, but before the war and for decades afterward, though the models and makes of the cars and pickup trucks changed dramatically, the art of cruising remained remarkably the same.

The attraction of the square was not limited to Lamar youth. It was perhaps even more appealing to teens and young adults from smaller neighboring communities, many of whom looked at Lamar, a city of about three thousand residents, as the big city and the square as a place of wonder.

Any Friday or Saturday night, it was easy to find young people from Golden City, seventeen miles to the east; Liberal, fourteen miles to the west; Jasper, twelve miles south; and even Lockwood, twenty-five miles east. And in the late 1930s, there was always a contingent from Sheldon, twelve miles north of Lamar, just past the Barton-Vernon County line.

One of those young people from Sheldon was a gregarious man who treated each person he met as if they were a good friend and the most important person in the world to him at that moment.

It was not pretense on Gerald Gilkey's part. From the beginning, he had a genuine interest in people and enjoyed being around them. People in Sheldon, Lamar and the surrounding communities knew who he was. But Gilkey's winning personality was not the only thing that made him stand out on the Lamar Square.

He was the only person anyone knew who had a canary yellow 1924 Model T.

It was standard-issue black when Gilkey bought the car for either seventeen or nineteen dollars from Gerald Beeny of Sheldon in 1938. It was his first car, and the sixteen-year-old wanted it to stand out.

Local law enforcement also knew who Gilkey was, though mostly for the same reason everyone else did. He was a likable young man. There were occasions, however, when the fun-loving Gilkey became quite a handful for law enforcement, including the time he and his friends tied a tire to the back of his car, set the tire afire and drove around the square.

Police officers shouted for Gilkey to go home, and he did. But he kept coming back until, eventually, he decided never to leave. Before he arrived in Lamar permanently, though, Gilkey embarked on ventures that took him far from the area.

After he graduated from Sheldon High School in 1939 at age seventeen, Gilkey attended college for one year at Kansas State Teachers College in Pittsburg, just across the Missouri-Kansas state line. After that, Gilkey and some friends decided to head west to seek their fortune.

For a time, Gilkey picked hops, but with the meager amount he earned, it was obvious he was not going to make his fortune any time soon. The next stop was Seattle, where Gilkey worked in a grocery store for a few months.

Finally, he returned home and found himself attracted to a player on the Sheldon High School girls' basketball team. "He asked if he could take me home after a game," Betty Gilkey recalled. Betty's parents, John and Lola Medlin, did not approve of this older man (Gilkey was twenty) pursuing their daughter.

"He was persistent," Betty said. "If he made up his mind, that's the way it was going to be." One time taking her home was going to be it, but Betty made sure it did not happen that way.

"I left my uniform in his car and he brought it back to me the next day." After that, the two were inseparable, much to the disapproval of her parents. Several months after they began seeing each other, they realized they wanted to spend their lives together. They decided to get married but told no one.

"My parents did not know we were getting married," Betty said. "I was still in high school."

The wedding took place on June 18, 1942, at the home of a minister friend in Webb City, about fifty miles south of Sheldon. "Gerald had carried the marriage license for two months," Betty said. It took only two days for the newlyweds' secret to be revealed in an item buried on page three of the June 20, 1942 *Joplin Globe*.

Headlined "Sheldon Couple Weds" and carrying a June 19 Webb City dateline, the news was broken to the Gilkey and Medlin families in this way: "Miss Betty Jo Medlin and Gerald W. Gilkey, both of Sheldon, Missouri, were married at 7 o'clock last night by Rev. Alfred E. Jenkins, pastor of the Emmanuel Baptist Church. The ceremony was performed in Jenkins' home on North Ball Street."

Betty's family reacted in an unexpected fashion. "They decided 'we're going to get behind them and we're going to help them,'" Betty said.

The Gilkeys were only able to enjoy being together for three months. In September 1942, Gerald Gilkey received his draft notice. He took his preliminary examination on September 25 in Springfield, then, on September 29, he was sworn into the U.S. Army. After their goodbyes, Betty Gilkey returned to Sheldon. "It was three years before I saw him again."

Betty Gilkey, still a newlywed when Gerald, after being drafted into the U.S. Army Air Force, was shipped to the Aleutians, was doing her part to help the war effort. She moved from Sheldon to Kansas City, where she worked for North America Aviation. "I wasn't a Rosie the Riveter," Betty said, "I worked in the offices, but I knew all of those girls. I talked to them every day."

Gerald Gilkey was far from the battle; he and the men who were in the Aleutians encountered a different kind of problem being stationed far away from home in a place where you were not going to get a two-week furlough to see the home folk.

Gilkey used a special talent to land one of the better jobs at his base, office manager. "He was one of the fastest typists they had," Gilkey's son Steve said, "so they put him in the office." While some men were unable to cope with the isolation, Gilkey had two hobbies to help him pass the time: photography and cutting hair.

That was Gilkey's existence as the war continued until early in 1945, when he was approved for a five-week furlough. It was not long after Gilkey arrived in Missouri that the news broke that the war was over and he learned that, while his country appreciated his services, it did not need them any longer.

Gilkey's personal things remained at the Aleutian base. "He never went back to pick up any of his belongings," Betty Gilkey said.

When he returned from his tour of duty, Gilkey used the money he had saved and bought an auto-parts business. After a couple of years, with the store not doing well and he and Betty having an infant son, Steve, he sold the business and went to work for his brothers-in-law, Jewell and Gerald Medlin, at an Oldsmobile dealership in Fort Scott, Kansas.

On the first day at his new job, Gilkey, a natural salesman, sold one of the highest-priced cars Oldsmobile made, an Olds 98. The Medlin brothers eventually decided they wanted to move closer to home and, in 1950, opened an Oldsmobile dealership in Lamar.

As the Medlins made arrangements to open the Lamar dealership, Gilkey remained in Fort Scott, charged with selling as many of the remaining fourteen cars on the lot as possible. He bought a full-page newspaper ad and radio time. Within eight days, all fourteen cars had been sold, and he was on his way to a new life in Lamar.

During the 1950s, Gilkey sold Oldsmobiles for the Medlin brothers and became a well-known and well-liked member of the community. As the decade neared an end, he was certain he wanted to own his own car dealership. The only thing that stood in his way was the knowledge that in order to do so, he and Betty would have to leave Lamar. Gilkey did not intend to compete for customers with his wife's family by buying one of the other car lots in the city.

In 1959, an opportunity of a different kind presented itself. Stan White, co-publisher of the *Democrat*, approached Gilkey about running for city council. After giving it much thought and consulting with his wife, Gilkey put his name into consideration and received the nomination of the Lamar Democratic Party during its caucus in the Barton County Courthouse.

The Ward One council seat was being vacated by Norbert Heim, the Democratic nominee for mayor, who was already assured of election because the city's Republicans at their caucus, which was also held at the courthouse, agreed to nominate the much-respected Heim despite his Democratic Party affiliation.

Gilkey was elected to the city council in April as one of two Ward One representatives. In that same month, he served as a member of the committee that welcomed Truman during dedication ceremonies for the Truman Birthplace.

As he settled into city government, Gilkey still held dreams of owning his own business and received a tempting offer from former mayor Loyd Gathman.

Gathman, who owned the Chevrolet dealership in Lamar, approached Gilkey about buying it. Though having his own dealership was something Gilkey dearly wanted, he rejected Gathman's proposal, because he felt it would be disloyal to the Medlins.

Shortly after that, he learned of an opportunity to buy a dealership in Abilene, Kansas. It was a difficult decision. In the ten years Gilkey had lived in Lamar, he had grown to love the city. He enjoyed the people, the sense of community and the feeling that he was contributing through his city council work.

He and Betty weighed the pros and cons of making the move. They would be moving away from their families and taking Steve out of his school and away from his friends. But this was what Gilkey had dreamed of doing since his first day in the auto-sales business, and they decided to pull the trigger and make the move to Abilene.

When Betty's brother Jewell Medlin learned what his brother-in-law was planning, he made a counteroffer. He would sell his dealership to Gilkey. Gilkey, two months into his second city council term, accepted the offer.

Gilkey contacted Gathman and closed a deal to buy the Chevrolet dealership. Gilkey Chevrolet opened at 902 Broadway. In July 1961, Gilkey became owner of the Chevrolet and Oldsmobile franchises for Lamar.

In 1965, after serving six years as mayor, Norbert Heim decided not to run for a fourth two-year term and asked Gilkey to consider running for the office. Gilkey had done more than just attend council meetings and vote. He had thrived on committee work and had a knack for smoothing over disagreements and solving problems.

In April 1965, Gilkey was elected mayor. From the beginning, and each day as the years passed, Lamar residents with problems made their way to Gilkey Chevrolet to seek help from the mayor or to express their anger over something that was happening in the city.

"We had people come in mad, slamming doors when they went into his office," his granddaughter Courtney Gardner said, "but by the time they came out they were laughing and best friends."

Gilkey's son Steve, who worked at the car dealership with his father, said there was an initial fear that Gilkey being mayor would have an adverse effect on the business, but it never did. "He had a way with people. They'd get mad at him as mayor, but not the person. They would keep doing business with him. I don't know how he did that."

The job occasionally crept into Gilkey's home life, as well. "He would get calls at night and he would talk to them," Betty recalled. "I just would not have had that patience."

Steve Gilkey remembered, "There was one lady who would call and say she had UFOs outside her window and ask him to send the police department down there." With that woman, as well as anyone else who called, Gilkey always listened.

One key to Gilkey's success as mayor of Lamar was the quality of the people working for him at his car dealership. Gilkey was comfortable leaving his staff, which included son Steve, in charge while he represented Lamar's interests at regional meetings in Joplin and Springfield, in front of state officials in Jefferson City and even in Washington, D.C. "It allowed Dad to do what he wanted to do," Steve Gilkey said. "He really loved politics."

Together with the city council, Gilkey steered Lamar through the most successful period in its history. Through an advantageous deal for purchasing electricity from the Southwest Power Administration, the city made enough money that in both 1983 and 1986, city residents received the holiday gift of no electric bills for the month of December.

The 1983 Christmas gift received national publicity from wire services and through a mention on the nationally syndicated Paul Harvey radio show.

More national attention came to Gerald and Steve Gilkey the following year, when Lamar became the first community in the nation in which the same owners operated both the Chevrolet and Ford dealerships.

Other successes for the city of Lamar while Gilkey was mayor included the area's first aquatic park and the construction of a performing arts auditorium. In addition, Gilkey, lobbying successfully along with Nell Finley, State Representative Jerry Burch and council members, stopped a state plan to cut the hours the Truman Birthplace remained open.

Every two years like clockwork, Gilkey filed for reelection. He served as mayor for thirty-six years, the longest time a person ever served as a mayor in Missouri history.

Counting his time on city council, he served the city for forty-two years. "He was never tempted to quit," Betty Gilkey said.

Gilkey's last council meeting was on April 16, 2001. When his final meeting adjourned, his successor as mayor, longtime city councilman Keith Divine, was sworn in. Among the new council members, representing Ward One, the same position Gilkey once held, was Steve Gilkey.

On July 17, 2006, one year after Gerald Gilkey's death, the Gilkey family attended a ceremony in the city's Thiebaud Auditorium unveiling a portrait of Lamar's longtime mayor.

Mayor Keith Divine said the portrait captured the Gerald Gilkey he had served with for twenty-three years, down to that "certain twinkle" in his eyes. Divine announced that the portrait would hang on the east wall of the Lamar City Hall lobby and that, when and if a new city hall was ever built, it would be named after Gerald Gilkey.

Betty Gilkey told the more than two hundred people who attended the ceremony: "The city was his love. He loved all the people."

DOROTHY STRATTON

After Harry Truman was sworn in as president following the death of Franklin D. Roosevelt on April 12, 1945, the city of Lamar was well represented among those leading the war effort.

In addition to Truman, who was commander in chief, Admiral Freeland Daubin, commander of the submarines in the Atlantic Fleet, and Admiral Charles Lockwood, who commanded the submarines in the Pacific, were both Lamar High School graduates, as was Admiral Thomas Selby Combs, who served as chief of staff for naval aircraft in the southwest Pacific.

Lamar's prominence was noted even before Truman received the vice-presidential nomination in an editorial titled "Lamar All Out for U.S. Navy" in the June 17, 1943 *Joplin Globe*.

In addition to Admirals Daubin and Lockwood and Combs, who was a captain at that time, the editorial noted that a woman with a Lamar connection was in charge of the newly established U.S. Coast Guard Women's Reserve, which played a key role in the war effort.

Dorothy Constance Stratton, born on March 27, 1899, in Brookfield, Missouri, was the daughter of Reverend Richard L. Stratton, a Baptist minister, and Anna (Troxler) Stratton.

The Strattons came to Lamar in 1911, when Richard became minister at the Baptist church. Dorothy spent the next three years living in a duplex, where her fondest memory was the cookies a neighbor shared with her. The family left Lamar after she attended Lamar High School for a year, and Dorothy graduated from high school in Blue Rapids, Kansas.

Of those early years in Lamar and Blue Rapids, Dorothy later recalled that, more than anything, she wanted to dance, but that was something Baptist girls were not allowed to do.

After high school, she attended Ottawa University, a private Baptist school in Ottawa, Kansas, where she received a bachelor of arts degree. After graduation, she was offered a job at an Ottawa newspaper. "It was mighty tempting," she told a *Kansas City Star* reporter in a February 1943 interview. "I always wanted to write." She opted instead to pursue a career in education.

She received a master's degree in psychology from the University of Chicago and later earned a doctorate in student personnel administration. Dorothy worked her way through her postgraduate degrees by teaching.

She spent six years as vice-principal and dean of girls at San Bernardino Senior High School in California before being hired as the first full-time dean of women at Purdue University in 1933.

When she took the position, only 500 women were attending Purdue, with many of them receiving degrees in home economics. By the time she left the post in 1942, more than 1,400 women attended the university and three women's residence halls had been built.

Stratton would likely have stayed at Purdue much longer, but she, like many other Americans, had her life changed on December 7, 1941, when the Japanese bombed Pearl Harbor. She took a leave of absence from her position at the university and volunteered to join the Women's Reserve of the U.S. Navy, better known as WAVES (Women Accepted for Voluntary Emergency Services).

A colleague of Dorothy's said, "You can't afford to do this."

She replied, "I can't afford not to."

Dorothy was commissioned as a lieutenant and, after training at Smith College in Northampton, Massachusetts, served as assistant to the commanding officer at the radio school for WAVES in Madison, Wisconsin, a position that did not last long. One evening, she was ordered to take the "fastest transportation possible" to Washington, D.C.

When she arrived, she met with three admirals and a commandant and learned that she had been promoted to lieutenant commander and selected to organize the U.S. Coast Guard Women's Reserve, which had been authorized in November 1942, when President Roosevelt signed an amendment to Public Law 773. She was transferred from the U.S. Navy to the Coast Guard, where she not only became the leader of the reserve but also the only person in it. One of her first accomplishments was to create a simple title for the reserve, similar to WAVES for the navy reserve.

Coast Guard officials were considering calling it WARLOGs, but Dorothy, combining the Coast Guard motto *Semper Paratus* and its English translation, "Always Ready," recommended SPARs, and that acronym was chosen.

She was modest about her title and rank in later years. "I'm sometimes referred to as the commanding officer of the SPARs. Actually, I had no command authority. All I had was the power of persuasion."

From the time she assumed the command of SPARs in 1942, through January 1946, she persuaded thousands of recruits and created a reserve that included eleven thousand women. In 1944, she was promoted to captain.

She received the Legion of Merit for her contribution to women in the military.

After the war, Dorothy became the first director of the International Monetary Fund, and in 1950, she became director of Girl Scouts of the U.S.A. She retired from that position in 1960.

In 2001, when Dorothy was 102, the U.S. Coast Guard's Women's Leadership Association named its Captain Dorothy Stratton Leadership Award in her honor, presenting the award "to a female officer of the Coast Guard who demonstrates leadership and mentorship and who shares the Coast Guard's core values."

Dorothy C. Stratton died on September 17, 2006, at age 107. Two years after her death, the Coast Guard named its third Legend-class cutter the USCGC *Stratton* (WMSL-752). It was the first Legend-class cutter named for a woman.

On July 23, 2010, First Lady Michelle Obama christened the cutter at the Ingalls Shipyard in Pascagoula, Mississippi. During her address prior to the christening, Obama recounted the work Stratton did with SPARs. "The SPARs were designed to free up men for the war. But it also freed a new generation of women to believe in themselves—as radio operators, air traffic controllers, parachute riggers and machinists."

The volunteers that Dorothy recruited during her years at SPARs also included African American women, the First Lady noted.

Obama reminded those in attendance of the words Stratton had spoken years after the war. "All we asked was for the Coast Guard just to give the women a chance."

"They gave the women the chance, and the women made good."

FREELAND DAUBIN

*T*he circumstances that placed three Lamar men in leadership ranks of the U.S. Navy would never have occurred had it not been for a speech given at Lamar High School in 1899.

The man who delivered that speech, Ensign Lloyd Shapley, was a Barton County native and older brother of Harlow Shapley (1885–1972), the noted astronomer and director of the Harvard College Observatory. At least one person, a thirteen-year-old at the time, was inspired enough by what he later described as Ensign Shapley's "fiery" speech to change the direction of his life.

Freeland Allyn Daubin was born on February 6, 1886, in Lamar, the son of Crittenden Clay Daubin and Ella Nettie Daubin. His father served sixteen years as Barton County treasurer.

After he heard Shapley's speech, Daubin was determined to join the navy. He was valedictorian of the Lamar High School class of 1903 and attended the University of Missouri in Columbia for one term, paying for his education by firing furnaces and waiting on tables at boardinghouses. He was elected president of the freshman class.

When the person who was appointed to the U.S. Naval Academy in 1905 failed to pass the physical, Daubin, still inspired by Shapley's speech, applied and received the appointment.

While he was at Annapolis, Daubin participated in track and was the associate editor of the *Lucky Bag*, a satirical annual magazine published by the U.S. Naval Academy's graduating class. Each year, each graduating student was described. Daubin received this description: "He's from Missouri and

The former German *U-111*, photographed at New York on April 17, 1919, at the time of its arrival from Plymouth, England. This vessel was handed over at Plymouth on April 1, 1919. Lieutenant Commander Freeland A. Daubin, USN, commanding officer of the former *U-111* until summer 1919, can be seen on deck amidships. *Naval History and Heritage Command.*

is perhaps as good a kicker as ever came from that mule-raising state. He is a man of quick mind and strong energetic temperament, always ready to shove a good thing along or sit on a bad one."

After his graduation in 1909, Daubin served on the battleships *North Carolina* and *Connecticut* and was appointed an ensign in 1911.

The following year exposed Daubin to the section of the U.S. Navy where he made his mark, as he entered the submarine service. His first command was the *C-4* in 1913.

An article Daubin published in the *Journal of the Naval Institute* in early 1917 received much attention. It detailed the contributions that submarines could make as units of the fleet, noting that the performance of the vessels during war games had demonstrated the capabilities they could provide to protect the nation's coastline.

In World War I, Daubin served as an aide on the staff of the commander of the Submarine Force of the Atlantic Fleet.

When the war ended, Daubin insisted that the British give a German submarine they had captured, the *U-111*, to the United States. It took only a few days for Daubin and an American crew to master the vessel's intricate equipment. His actions also enabled the Americans to gain much knowledge about the construction and operation of German submarines.

After serving on submarines from 1912 to 1924, Daubin served on destroyers and battleships for the next fifteen years, returning to the submarine service in 1939. In 1941, he took command of the submarine fleet at Pearl Harbor. He was given a temporary promotion to rear admiral in November 1941. Under Daubin's leadership, not one submarine was lost during the Japanese attack on December 7, 1941.

Following the attack, Daubin stepped in to prevent a grounded Japanese midget submarine from being destroyed, convincing his superiors that the characteristics and capabilities of the vessel could be explored, providing the United States with valuable information as it entered war with Japan.

In March 1942, he was named commander of the submarines for the Atlantic Fleet and was permanently promoted to rear admiral on June 30, 1942.

Though most of the submarine warfare was taking place in the Pacific Ocean, Daubin's position essentially enabled him to determine the quality of all of those who were in the submarine service.

The Atlantic commander's job was to oversee construction, repairs and testing of all submarines, conduct trial runs and provide training for all of those who would see action in the Atlantic and Pacific.

From left to right: General George C. Marshall, Eleanor Roosevelt, Fleet Admiral Ernest King and Rear Admiral Freeland A. Daubin at the launch of USS *Franklin D. Roosevelt* (CV-42) in April 1945. *Naval History and Heritage Command.*

In a March 31, 1943 speech in New London, Connecticut, Daubin provided an overview of his job, how the war effort was going and what type of men were welcomed into the submarine service.

"Our subs need good, tough men," he said, "men with physical stamina. The character of submarine service is peculiar. For battles between surface ships, the engagement lasts about thirty seconds and sailors can key themselves up to it in advance. The same applies to air battles to a certain extent.

"In submarines, the men go on patrols lasting many weeks and 90 percent of them never see the sun during this time. Sometimes the tables are reversed, and they are themselves attacked by depth charges and other weapons."

Though Daubin painted a grim picture of the lives of those in the submarine service, there was something about the job that made it worthwhile, he said. "The main attraction is that they get a chance to sink Japanese ships."

In February 1945, Daubin received the Navy Distinguished Service Medal.

Daubin remained commander of the Atlantic Fleet until December 5, 1946, when he was appointed commandant of the Navy Yard in Brooklyn, New York, a position he held until 1948.

After spending nearly four decades in the navy, Daubin retired in 1948, spending his final years in California. He died at Bethesda Naval Hospital on October 24, 1959, at age seventy-three.

CHARLES LOCKWOOD

*T*he impassioned speech Ensign Lloyd Shapley delivered in 1899 indirectly influenced another Lamar High School graduate to submit his application for the U.S. Naval Academy.

Charles Andrews Lockwood Jr. was born on May 6, 1890, the son of Midland, Virginia businessman Charles Andrews Lockwood and Flora C. Lockwood. The family moved to Lamar, where Charles Lockwood Sr. established himself in business and later served as mayor.

The younger Lockwood attended Lamar High School, briefly crossing paths with the older Freeland Daubin. When Lockwood graduated in 1908, Daubin encouraged him to apply for the Naval Academy.

Lockwood received the appointment and while in Annapolis excelled in track, lettering and breaking the school record for the one-mile run. When the annual satirical magazine the *Lucky Bag* was published in his senior year, in 1912, Lockwood was described as "a simon-pure tough nut who would rather do something real devilish than be president or have five stripes."

After serving briefly on the USS *Mississippi* and USS *Arkansas*, a lifelong association with submarines began in 1914 for Ensign Lockwood. In a brief tour as an instructor in the Naval Training Station, Great Lakes, he reported to the USS *Mohican* for submarine instruction. He later held posts at Shanghai and with the Yangtze Patrol Force.

Lockwood received his first submarine command, USS *A-2*, followed by service on USS *B-1*. During World War I, he served as commander of Submarine Division 1, Asiatic Fleet.

After the war, Lockwood was in London with Lieutenant Freeland Daubin. While Daubin was leading an American crew back to the United States with a captured German submarine, Lockwood was doing the same, commanding the crew that brought the *UC-97* to the States.

Among his assignments between the two world wars, Lockwood served in the Naval Yard at Portsmouth, New Hampshire; was assistant chief of the U.S. Naval Mission to Brazil between 1928 and 1931; and taught seamanship and navigation at the U.S. Naval Academy.

In June 1939, he was assigned to the light cruiser USS *Richmond* as chief of staff to Commander Submarine Force, U.S. Fleet, and in February 1941, he was assigned to London as principal observer of submarines.

The course of Lockwood's career changed with the bombing of Pearl Harbor. He immediately cabled the Navy Department and asked for submarine duty in the Pacific. That request was accommodated.

Lockwood was promoted to rear admiral in June 1942, becoming the second Lamar High School graduate to achieve that rank. After a plane crash in February 1943 in California killed Rear Admiral Robert Henry English, Commander of Submarines for the Pacific Fleet (COMSUBPAC), Lockwood was transferred to that post and in November of that year was promoted to vice admiral.

In his new post, Lockwood implemented improvements in the leadership and weaponry of the vessels under his command. He revitalized crews by removing skippers who were unwilling to put themselves in harm's way and replacing them with younger, more forceful leaders who would take the war to the Japanese.

In addition, Lockwood quickly developed a reputation as a leader who put his men first. Recognizing the stress that spending weeks undersea could put on the submariners, he provided them two weeks of rest and recuperation at the Royal Hawaiian Hotel in Honolulu.

When his men returned from missions in which their only food was packaged military rations, Lockwood made sure they were greeted with ice cream and fresh vegetables.

Charles A. Lockwood, vice admiral, USN, is shown aboard a navy submarine in May 1945. *Naval History and Heritage Command, National Archives.*

Lockwood made sure the men under his command were provided the tools to allow them to succeed. In addition to assigning new leaders with fresh perspectives, Lockwood replaced outdated vessels with newly constructed fleet submarines directly from American shipyards.

More bases were added, including in the Philippines and Guam, enabling submarine crews to reduce the length of their missions.

Just as important, Lockwood was willing to do battle with others in the naval hierarchy to guarantee his men had the best weaponry available. Rear Admiral Ralph Waldo Christie insisted that U.S. submarines continue to use the Mark 14 torpedo and the Mark 6 exploder. Christie had a hand in developing those weapons, and though they had not been effective against Japanese submarines, he insisted the problem was not with the devices but with the men who were using them. Lockwood conducted tests showing the flaws in the weapons and replaced them with improved torpedoes.

Armed with better leaders, better weapons and better morale, it did not take long for the Pacific Fleet to gain the upper hand over the Japanese. Controlling a fleet of 100 submarines, 4,000 officers and 48,000 men, Lockwood's fleet sank 1,182 Japanese merchant ships and 314 naval vessels while rescuing 504 airmen. Lockwood's fleet lost only 52 submarines.

Lockwood assessed the performance of his fleet succinctly in a 1955 interview. "The sea was planted with Japanese boats."

Lockwood, the man who more than anyone else was responsible for that success, never fired a torpedo during his nearly four decades in the navy.

After the war, Lockwood served as naval inspector general and planted the seeds for modern U.S. submarines. After being invited to a 1946 conference in which the construction of the submarines of the future was being considered, Lockwood pushed for the use of atomic power to create the most powerful submarine afloat, leading to the construction of the USS *Nautilus*, the first nuclear submarine, launched on January 21, 1954.

Following his retirement in June 1947, Lockwood embarked on a second career as an author, writing military history books, particularly about submarines. The lengthy list of his nonfiction books include *Tragedy at Honda*; *Sink 'Em All*; *Through Hell and Deep Water*; *Hell at 50 Fathoms*; *Zoomies, Subs and Zeros*; *Battles of the Philippine Sea*; and his autobiography, *Down to the Sea in Subs: My Life in the U.S. Navy*.

Perhaps his best-known book, published in 1955, was *Hellcats of the Sea*, in which he detailed the work done by the Pacific Submarine Fleet during World War II. Columbia Pictures purchased the rights to the book, changed the name to *Hellcats of the Navy* and used Lockwood as a technical adviser on the film.

Vice Admiral Charles A. Lockwood, USN (Ret.), is shown at the periscope of the USS *Nautilus* off San Francisco, June 24, 1957. Fleet Admiral Chester W. Nimitz and other submarine admirals were also onboard, taking their first cruise on a nuclear submarine. *Naval History and Heritage Command, National Archives.*

Hellcats of the Navy, a fictionalized version of Lockwood's book, starred future president Ronald Reagan and his wife, Nancy Davis, the only time the two appeared in a movie together.

Submarine movies were popular in the 1950s, and Lockwood served as a technical adviser on many, including *Operation Pacific* (1951), starring John Wayne, Patricia Neal and Ward Bond; *On the Beach* (1959), a post–nuclear war film starring Gregory Peck, Ava Gardner and Fred Astaire; *Up Periscope* (1959), starring James Garner and Edmond O'Brien; and *Torpedo Run* (1958), featuring Glenn Ford and Ernest Borgnine.

Lockwood spent his retirement raising prunes on a six-acre farm in Los Gatos, California, south of San Francisco. He died on June 7, 1967, at age seventy-seven.

THOMAS SELBY COMBS

*T*he unlikely ascension of three Lamar High School graduates to positions in the upper hierarchy of the U.S. Navy was spelled out in the opening paragraph of an Associated Press article published on June 17, 1943. "There was no reason to expect that Lamar would prove a flowering bed for the Navy. Barton County has neither rivers nor lakes and the only ponds are formed by rain gathering in the pits of strip coal mines. The water supply is drilled from wells. Yet in addition to the careers of Admirals Daubin and Lockwood, Lamar has grown into a nautical center of no mean proportions."

Though that article concentrated on Daubin and Lockwood, it also noted Dorothy C. Stratton, who at that time was the recently appointed director of the Women's Reserve of the U.S. Coast Guard and the most recent addition to Lamar's collection of admirals.

The youngest of Lamar's three admirals, Thomas Selby Combs, was born on March 25, 1898, the first of three sons of Orin P. Combs and Grace M. Combs. Though Combs, like Charles Lockwood before him, received encouragement from Freeland Daubin to apply to the U.S. Naval Academy, dedication to public service was a hallmark of the Combs family.

Orin Combs served six terms as mayor of Lamar. Both of Thomas Combs's brothers became lawyers; Carol Combs also served as Lamar mayor and Barton County prosecuting attorney.

Thomas Combs graduated from Lamar High School in 1915, a classmate of Charles Lockwood's younger brother Arthur. After Ensign Combs served

Vice Admiral Thomas Selby Combs. *National Archives.*

on the battleship USS *Kansas* during World War I, he graduated from the U.S. Naval Academy in 1920. During the 1920s, he served on the USS *Florida*, USS *Minnesota*, USS *Connecticut* and USS *Nevada*.

After spending much of the 1930s serving aboard the carrier *Saratoga* and as squadron commander of the carrier *Enterprise*, the seasoned Combs was prepared for the challenges he would face during World War II, when he was promoted to rear admiral in 1943 and became chief of staff for aircraft in the southwest Pacific.

In 1944 and 1945, Combs was commander of the USS *Yorktown* during its successful campaign against the Japanese, which earned him the Distinguished Service Medal. He also earned the Silver Star, which he received on July 6, 1945, and the Legion of Merit on November 20, 1945.

After the war, Combs served as chief of staff to the commander of the Seventh Fleet (1945–46), deputy chief of the Bureau of Aeronautics (1946–48), commander of a carrier division (1949–50) and then chief of staff to the commander in chief of the Atlantic Fleet (1953–54), when he was promoted to vice admiral.

Combs commanded the Sixth Fleet in the Mediterranean (1954–55), served as deputy chief of naval operations for air (1956–58) and completed his career on March 31, 1960, while holding more command titles (five) than any active American naval officer.

- Commander, Atlantic Reserve Fleet, which included ships and the Eastern and Gulf Seaboards
- Commander, Eastern Sea Frontier, including forty states and extending forty miles to sea
- Commandant, Third Naval District, including New York, Connecticut and northern New Jersey
- Commander, U.S. Naval Base in New York, including the shipyard and the Naval Ammunition Depot in Earle, New Jersey
- U.S. Naval Representative, Military Staff Committee, United Nations

Before his retirement, Combs was honored with the Gray Eagle Award, presented to the naval aviator who had been on active duty for the longest continual period of time.

On March 29, 1960, Combs received a Gold Star in lieu of a second Distinguished Service Medal.

Thomas Selby Combs retired to Tallahassee, Florida, where he died of a heart attack on December 10, 1964, at age sixty-six. He is buried in Arlington National Cemetery.

TOM O'SULLIVAN

*I*n the months following the conclusion of World War II, Lamar civic leaders, armed with a considerable amount of land and a railroad spur connecting with the Frisco and Missouri Pacific lines, launched a search for a manufacturing company willing to move to the city and provide well-paying jobs to city and area residents.

The Industrial Committee was formed in 1946, and its first success came a year later, when Springfield businessman Ted Hutchens, president of Hutchens Metal Products, agreed to move a portion of his company to Lamar if the city would loan him $120,000 to buy a site and build a factory. The loan would be repaid over ten years with no interest.

A fundraising drive netted $100,000 in less than a month, enough to convince Hutchens to begin the paperwork, but by the end of the year, he backed out, though it did not take long for the two sides to renew talks.

During a January 26, 1948 public meeting at Memorial Hall, Hutchens and the Industrial Committee unveiled a plan for an even bigger plant at a cost of $125,000. To show good faith, Hutchens deposited $20,000 in the Industrial Committee's account.

The 62,000-square-foot factory, including a 400-by-125-foot concrete-and-steel building, was erected between March and September 1948 at 1900 Gulf. Though Hutchens's business was not in Lamar long, his decision to relocate part of his business to the city and the construction of the factory laid the groundwork for industrial success in the city for the remainder of the century.

The next tenant at 1900 Gulf was the J.G. Doyle Engineering Company, a lawn mower manufacturer that needed a larger location and was still reeling from the effects of a fire that destroyed its plant in Grandview, Missouri. Owner Jack Doyle bought the Lamar facility in 1950, offering immediate employment to two hundred and a $300,000 boost to the economy.

A bitter divorce battle forced Doyle to sell his company in 1952, and the plant eventually became the Lawn-Boy division of the Outboard Marine and Manufacturing Company. Over the next eleven years, it more than doubled the number of employees.

Without any notice, Outboard Marine and Manufacturing president W.C. Scott issued a brief news release on Monday, July 8, 1963, announcing that the Lamar facility would close in October.

Even top officials in Lamar had not been told of the closing, Mayor Norbert Heim told the *Joplin Globe*. A Lawn-Boy official called Heim at 11:30 a.m. and asked him to attend a 2:00 p.m. meeting. Four representatives from Outboard Marine and Manufacturing's home base read a brief announcement of the plant's impending closure.

"No one in Lamar had any idea of the plant being closed," Heim said. The Industrial Development Committee immediately launched a search and, for the next several months, had prospects, but none panned out. The search eventually led to a businessman whose success would end any regrets about the loss of Lawn-Boy.

Thomas Marshall O'Sullivan was born on December 19, 1921, in Doe Run, Missouri, the youngest of ten children of Daniel and Katie Williams O'Sullivan. At age twenty-four, he established his first business, Kirkwood Machine and Manufacturing in Kirkwood, Missouri, a community of eighteen thousand in St. Louis County.

At its height, O'Sullivan Industries in Lamar, founded by Tom O'Sullivan, employed more than 1,200 people. *O'Sullivan family photo.*

O'Sullivan was a well-organized businessman who kept a notebook of all of his deals, planned projects and ideas. "He reviewed his notes religiously before dinner each night then when he met with others, he often knew the answers before the questions were asked." his daughter Betty Thieman said.

During the Korean War, O'Sullivan landed government contracts building machine castings for bombs, leading to construction of a larger factory. When combat ceased in July 1953, the contracts ended.

The idea for the company that would eventually bear Tom O'Sullivan's name came at a July 4 picnic, according to *Simply the Best: The O'Sullivan Story*, the company history published in 2000.

> *During an Independence Day cookout, O'Sullivan's neighbor was struggling to move his portable television from his living room to his patio for the party. The neighbor remarked that someone should make a stand for the new portable television. It sparked an idea in O'Sullivan and the next day he began constructing a wrought iron television stand, possibly the world's first portable television stand.*

O'Sullivan built the prototype in his home machine shop and was excited about the prospect of manufacturing and selling the stands, but he was concerned about the stability of the manufacturing industry, something he had just experienced with the end of the Korean conflict.

O'Sullivan had family members who were involved in the nursing-home industry, and he considered buying a nursing home in Sullivan, Missouri, approximately seventy miles southwest of St. Louis.

While he was in Sullivan, O'Sullivan was told there was a vacant factory building in the small town of Japan, eight miles east. O'Sullivan reached an agreement with the building's owner, George Koelling, leased the facility and moved his family from Kirkwood to Sullivan to begin his new venture.

The creation of the television stand was just the first innovation for O'Sullivan. To eliminate burdensome shipping and freight costs, Sullivan Industries made ready-to-assemble stands. The products were pitched to the two biggest television manufacturing companies, Westinghouse and General Electric.

A dispute with Koelling, who felt the heavy machinery used in the manufacturing process was damaging his building, led to an agreement that O'Sullivan would leave the building by February 1, 1957, something he was planning to do anyway, as the business was growing and lacked room to expand in Japan.

Though Sullivan offered property that could be used, O'Sullivan moved his business to Owensville, twenty-four miles northwest of Japan, and the business was renamed O'Sullivan Industries. At Owensville, the company quickly expanded to seventy employees, was making five hundred units per week and was selling them to General Electric, Philco and Top Value Stamps.

During the time in Owensville, O'Sullivan Industries began to develop into a family business, as Tom O'Sullivan's oldest son, Dan, began working at the factory for thirty cents an hour and received a raise when the government pointed out to his father that the minimum wage was fifty cents an hour, according to *Simply the Best*.

The growth of O'Sullivan Industries ran into a potential roadblock in late 1959, when the United Steel Workers mounted an effort to unionize the factory. "If a labor union does go in and insists that I pay city-scale wages, it will be economically impossible to keep operating in Owensville," O'Sullivan told the city's newspaper, the *Owensville-Gasconade County Republican*.

O'Sullivan and the Owensville Industrial Corporation (OIC) combined to successfully thwart the unionization effort, with considerable help from the newspaper, which published a page-one article on January 28, 1960, headlined "OIC Concerned over Possible Loss of Local Industry," with a smaller headline beneath it, "O'Sullivan Can Be Forced to Move."

On February 5, 1960, 120 of O'Sullivan Industries' 150 employees voted against the union. In the next issue of the *Owensville-Gasconade County Republican*, O'Sullivan bought an advertisement to express his appreciation.

> *I wish to take this opportunity to thank my employees for their support and for their confidence in O'Sullivan Industries during the recent vote here. In the future, I will make every effort to attempt to merit your support and confidence and to make our employer-employee relationship one of the best.*

After the union election, O'Sullivan Industries continued to grow, so much so that it had to build on to its Owensville plant. By 1964, it had also opened a plant in Moberly, Missouri.

One of the reasons for the company's growth was the addition of Daniel O'Sullivan in sales and marketing. The younger O'Sullivan, who began working full-time for the company at age twenty-one in 1962, was instrumental in finding new outlets for O'Sullivan products, including Montgomery Ward and Sears, to go along with General Electric, RCA, J.C. Penney and Top Value.

It was obvious to Tom O'Sullivan that he needed even more property and access to more workers. A friend of O'Sullivan's who lived in Sullivan had a solution to the problem. Gerald Medlin, who was originally from Lamar, was aware of the problems his hometown had been having since the closing of the Lawn-Boy plant and thought the buildings, the room for future expansion, the proximity to the railroad spur and a sufficient workforce would be the answer to O'Sullivan's problems.

On August 21, 1964, O'Sullivan called Wayne Wirts, a member of Lamar's Industrial Development Committee, and two days later made his first visit to the city and found himself impressed both with the plant and with Lamar. On August 31, O'Sullivan, representatives of Outboard Manufacturing and a contingent from Lamar that included Heim, City Attorney Gordon Boyer and Industrial Development Committee members Wirts, Paul Kidwell and Henry Lisle met for five hours.

At the conclusion of the meeting, O'Sullivan had a handshake deal with Outboard Manufacturing to buy the former Lawn-Boy plant. For Lamar officials who had gone a year without being able to find a replacement for Lawn-Boy, the deal was a godsend. Tom and Betty O'Sullivan and their seven children made the move to the city.

Heim told the *Joplin Globe* that the workers for Lamar would be a perfect fit for O'Sullivan Industries' needs. "It shouldn't take an awful lot of training for the people to do the work. We feel we are fortunate in getting a plant such as this. They chose a good time to come."

By the end of the year, O'Sullivan Industries' new plant, which opened in October with thirty employees, had increased its workforce to two hundred. The plants in Owensville and Moberly were closed.

What the people of Lamar discovered quickly was that Tom O'Sullivan brought much more than jobs into the community. He put his money into community projects and offered a helping hand to people in need. "He found pleasure in helping the 'little guy' because he had been the little guy," O'Sullivan's daughter Betty Thieman said. "Many small businesses in our area were financed by him or others. He had an uncanny ability to get people to lead the way to give the community support."

O'Sullivan took an active role in finding those who needed help, keeping in touch with the pastors of local churches. "He truly cared about people," Thieman said.

For the remainder of the century, O'Sullivan Industries was a success story, with every move made by Tom and his management team resulting in greater sales and more employees. In 1969, O'Sullivan merged with Conroy, a fellow furniture manufacturer. The deal made Lamar residents anxious; for the first time, it left the O'Sullivan family without controlling interest in the company. But the concerns faded quickly as sales continued to grow rapidly through the 1970s, leading the company to expand the Lamar plant in 1979 from 146,000 square feet to 674,000.

At that point, a new problem was created. O'Sullivan Industries was still adding employees, but there was not enough housing in Lamar to handle the growth. That led to the creation of O'Sullivan Properties. Tom O'Sullivan bought land and worked with the Federal Housing Administration and Lamar area contractors to build new houses.

O'Sullivan Properties also bought existing houses when they came on the market and renovated them, creating rental units. With the housing problem solved, the population of Lamar, which had remained steady at about three thousand since the beginning of the century, grew to more than four thousand. O'Sullivan and his management team, using the same innovative approach that led to his creation of the TV stand in 1954, anticipated the needs of the time, expanding in the 1980s to build microwave oven carts and stands for TV and video games, computers and videocassette recorders.

In addition to O'Sullivan Properties, Tom and his wife established the Tom and Betty O'Sullivan Tandy Scholarships to Southwest Missouri State University (later Missouri State University) in Springfield. The scholarships went to any graduating senior who had a parent who worked at O'Sullivan Industries.

O'Sullivan's generosity benefited projects for many of Lamar's churches, funded the purchase of land and construction of a building for Barton County Senior Citizens, helped restore the Plaza Theater on the Lamar Square and paid for the tennis courts at Lamar High School. Much of the computer furniture at the Lamar schools also came from O'Sullivan Industries.

The community spirit was also evident in Tom and Betty O'Sullivan's children. In 1984, daughter Peggy Hillman served as the head of a steering committee that convinced Lamar R-1 School District voters to approve a bond issue for a new high school. The issue had failed in two previous elections.

Conroy sold O'Sullivan Industries to the Tandy Corporation in 1983, and in 1986, Tom O'Sullivan stepped down from his day-to-day role at the company he created, turning it over to his son Daniel, who continued to steer the company successfully through the remainder of the 1980s and 1990s, with sales growing to $380 million annually and new facilities opened in Cedar City, Utah, and South Boston, Virginia. The elder O'Sullivan continued his work with O'Sullivan Properties.

While O'Sullivan Industries remained profitable, Tandy was a troubled company. It made one of its few successful moves in 1994, when it decided to have a public offering of O'Sullivan Industries stock. The offering raised

$350 million, four times Tandy's initial investment. O'Sullivan appeared to be on a path to continued success.

The business climate was changing by the beginning of the twenty-first century, however, and several of O'Sullivan Industries' biggest customers, including Montgomery Ward, Venture and Best Products, declared bankruptcy and closed. Prices for materials the company needed increased, cutting deeply into profits.

American furniture makers were facing increased competition from inferior but cheaper foreign goods that were flooding the market. By 1996, though Daniel O'Sullivan remained chairman and CEO, Rick Davidson, formerly of Sunbeam Products, was the company's new president.

O'Sullivan Industries paid tribute to its founder by funding a project to refurbish the Lamar High School football stadium and name it after Tom O'Sullivan. The announcement that the stadium would become Thomas M. O'Sullivan Stadium, which took place prior to an October 1997 homecoming game, was carefully scripted, but the spur-of-the-moment and unplanned ceremony after the game meant even more to the man who was being honored.

The outcome of the Lamar-Monett game was in doubt until late in the fourth quarter, when a Lamar player tackled a Monett runner, preventing a game-tying two-point conversion.

When the game ended, the coach and players decided to give the game ball to Tom O'Sullivan. The player who made the game-saving tackle, O'Sullivan's grandson Jim Hillman, handed him the ball.

The game ball presentation meant as much to Hillman as it did to his grandfather. Hillman told the *Carthage Press*, "I have such a feeling of respect for him. He had absolutely nothing when he started, and he worked hard for everything he got."

When Tom O'Sullivan died on March 12, 2004, O'Sullivan Industries, the mainstay of Lamar's economy for four decades, was struggling to stay afloat. Five years earlier, OSI Acquisitions, an investment group, had purchased the company. On October 14, 2005, company officials filed for bankruptcy, saying they fully intended to restructure and emerge stronger. With no real plan and no visionary like Tom O'Sullivan to steer the ship, the recovery never took place.

Two years later, O'Sullivan Industries was out of business.

THE BROTHERHOOD

*F*ollowing the closing of O'Sullivan Industries, the city of Lamar launched a search for a new manufacturer to take over the facilities at 1900 Gulf.

Only a few months after O'Sullivan Industries closed, Dallas, Texas businessman Evan Daniels agreed to lease a portion of the plant and eventually hire 475 workers for his company, Polymer-Wood Technologies. Though that was far from the 1,200 O'Sullivan employed, the news offered hope for Lamar.

Daniels, however, had a checkered history. His previous business, Trio Industries, filed for bankruptcy, and on October 1, 2005, in the U.S. District Court for the Southern District of New York, Daniels's former partner, Robert Gyemant, accused Daniels of "theft of corporate property, unjust enrichment, misappropriation of trade secrets and tortious interference."

Trio Industries' bankruptcy ended the hopes of officials in Kalamazoo, Michigan, and Greenville, Mississippi, who had been told Trio would open facilities in their cities.

After Daniels showed his initial interest in Lamar and kept the lease on the building, months and then years passed, and while he hired a lobbyist, he never hired workers. Lamar's hopes of having a single manufacturer that would rescue the community were dashed.

Duncan Gepner runs for big yardage during Lamar High School's victory in the 2017 Class 2A State Championship game. Also shown are T.W. Ayers (41) and Caleb Gouge (69). *Photo by Terry Redman.*

Lamar residents found themselves forced to find jobs in other communities, with many commuting to Joplin, forty miles south, or to Pittsburg, Kansas, thirty miles west. Despite the lack of available jobs in the city, as the years passed, while some residents left, the community's population remained remarkably stable.

Still, the closing of O'Sullivan Industries and the departure of other businesses struck a heavy blow to community spirit, one that was finally reversed in the refurbished Lamar High School football stadium, which had been named after Tom O'Sullivan.

THERE WERE FEW LAMAR High School football teams in the 1970s and 1980s that did not have a Bailey on the roster.

Henry and Esther Bailey did not have an easy life, but they had a rewarding one. While Henry worked in the field, Esther was a "fried chicken, mashed potatoes and gravy" cooking mother of twelve, five boys and seven girls, according to a *Lamar Democrat* feature on the family published in 1989 when the youngest child, Steven, was preparing to graduate.

The Baileys' next-youngest child, Scott, graduated from Lamar High School in 1985 and attended Pittsburg State University on a football scholarship. "Scott made such good grades," Esther Bailey said. "He disciplined himself. It was inside of himself to do this."

After his graduation from Pittsburg State, Scott Bailey worked at a couple of engineering jobs and at O'Sullivan Industries and finally settled into banking, working ten years in Adrian, Missouri, and two years in Kirksville.

In addition to banking, Bailey returned to football, coaching the Miami-Amoret team to the state title game in 2001.

In 2002 and 2003, while Bailey was working at the Kirksville bank, he joined the coaching staff at Truman State University under Coach John Ware.

When Ware accepted the head-coaching position at Missouri Southern State University in Joplin, he convinced Bailey to leave banking behind and join him as a full-time assistant, a job he held through 2005 but that ended due to Ware's untimely death at age forty-six.

In 2006, Bailey returned to his hometown as the head coach of the Lamar High School football team, inheriting a talented senior-dominated team and guiding it to an 8-4 record and the state quarterfinals.

Without those seniors, most of whom had played on both offense and defense, the inexperienced Lamar Tigers fell to 0-10 the following year.

"If I had to do it over again," Bailey said, "I would have played more of the younger players on the varsity. We had a whole lot of guys taking reps on both sides of the ball and if you look at our best years when we're winning fifteen games and going undefeated, we had very few players playing on both sides of the ball."

Another problem with the 2007 team, Bailey said, was the offense he had the team running. "It was the offense I knew best; it was not the offense our kids did best."

Bailey said: "I was trying to fit them to me. I had to find out what they did best. I had to change."

At the beginning of the track and baseball seasons in the spring of 2008, the juniors from the winless football team asked to meet with Bailey. "I told Donna [Bailey's wife], 'they're going to quit. They know that last season was a huge failure, and they don't want to do it again.'"

The meeting was held the following day in Bailey's classroom. "I remember the start of the meeting they were all looking down at the desks and real quiet not saying anything. I finally spoke first and I said, 'You all asked for this meeting' and I asked them to speak up."

Lamar head coach Scott Bailey talks to his team during the 2012 Missouri 2A State Championship Game at the Edward Jones Dome in St. Louis. Pictured are seniors Jade Morgan (42) and Chad Rice (8). *Photo by Terry Redman.*

Clayton Rice was the first player to look up and broke the silence, saying, "Coach, all we want to know is how to win again."

At that point, Bailey showed the team the "spin" offense he and his coaching staff had devised for the 2008 season, an offense that would help overcome the size disadvantage his team had against other teams in the Big Eight Conference. It would depend on fakes and misdirection. "We kind of developed the saying, 'One good fake is worth two blocks.'"

The players bought into the new concept. "It gave the kids something that was unique, that they could call their own, that nobody else was really doing and if they could make it work—it was theirs. It was something that they owned."

In 2008, Lamar, the smallest school in the Big Eight, posted a 2-5 conference record, then won the first playoff game and lost the second. It was in that year that Bailey's younger brother Steven, an assistant coach, first referred to the team as the "Brotherhood" and emphasized the concept, which took hold the following year in the playoffs, when the Tigers became the first Lamar team to reach the state semifinals, where they lost to Maryville, 21-7, due to two turnovers that turned into touchdowns.

When Maryville easily defeated its opponent in the state championship game, Bailey began receiving phone calls from his players. "That was the time our kids realized that a state championship was doable."

The next year, Lamar again reached the state semifinals, playing top-ranked Maplewood. Lamar trailed, 20–19, early in the fourth quarter before Maplewood scored two late touchdowns to win, 33–19.

With two runs at a state championship falling just short, Lamar players and the community were already talking about the 2011 season. Jared Beshore, a freshman at the time of the Maplewood loss, remembered, "You walked around town and everyone was talking about football."

The heavily anticipated season did not disappoint Lamar fans. In the final game of the 2011 season, Lamar defeated Lafayette County–Higginsville, 49–19, at the Edward Jones Dome in St. Louis to win the Class 2A championship.

The winning continued year after year as Lamar defeated Blair Oaks (69–41) in 2012, Lawson (42–0) in 2013, South Callaway (30–15) in 2014, Malden (37–0) in 2015, Trinity Catholic (26–18) in 2016 and Lafayette County (37–20) in 2017.

The seven consecutive championships set a Missouri state record. At one point during the streak, Lamar had the longest active winning streak in U.S. high school football (fifty-seven games) from 2014 until the team lost in 2018.

Bailey remained with the team through 2019, when he resigned.

For his replacement, the Lamar R-1 School District did not have to leave the Brotherhood, hiring Branson assistant coach Jared Beshore, who had played on the 2011–13 Lamar state championship teams.

In 2020, Beshore's first season, the Brotherhood returned to the state championship game and earned Lamar its eighth banner, posting a 6–3 win over St. Pius X of Kansas City.

The Brotherhood's run came at a time when Lamar needed a lift, Beshore said. "Coach Bailey told us this town needed a light and we could be that light. We bought into that.

"We took pride in that."

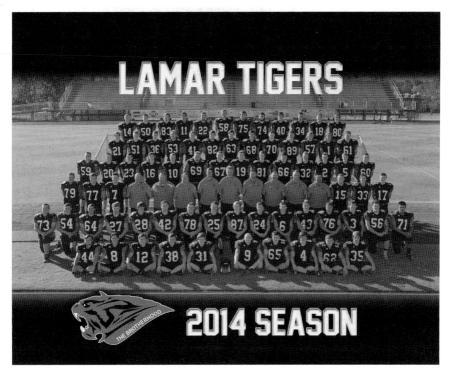

Members of the 2014 Missouri Class 2A state champion Lamar Tigers included the following: Derek Henderson, Alex Beetler, Tripp Tucker, Ben Kluhsman, Brett McDonald, Lakin Hardman, Colton Divine, Johnny Brooks, Cody Davis, Trenton Mooney, Angus Sprenkle, Riley Williams, Clayton Buzzard, John Rice, Dylan Robertson, Todd Morrow, Daniel Brisbin, Wyatt Davis, Thomas Mayfield, Danny Embry, Ryan Seaton, James White, Lincoln Kaderly, Jed Stahl, Keegan Duncan, Michael McWilliams, Chase McLane, Stanley Hunt, Alex Oden, Derek Parker, Rylee Cunningham, Jaycee Cornell, Matt Whyman, Sam Timmons, Tanner Phipps, James Givens, Luke Hardman, Hunter Gepner, Dylan Whitehead, Tristen Foster, Trey Mooney, Anthony Wilkerson, Sam Buzzard, Keegan Jones, Will Jeffries, Dru Finley, J.D. Allen, Bryce Mason, Kendall Morrow, Angel Contreras, Kyler Overstreet, Corwin Williams, McKade Crockett, Rick Middleton, Aaron Moenning, Cooper Lucas, Isaiah Cleveland, Mike Jones, Stuart McKarus, Michael Danner, Dalton Hasson, T.W. Ayers, Nick Gardner, Lane Fanning, Colby Fink, Hayden Bartholomew, Seth Fullerton, Hunter Bayless, Andrew Hillman, Chase McKibben and Brian Wilhelm. Head coach: Scott Bailey; assistant coaches: Thad Lundine, Steve Bailey, Glen Cox, Brett Pettibon and Chris Wilkerson. *Lamar High School photo.*

Members of the 2015 Missouri Class 2A state champion Lamar Tigers included the following: Todd Morrow, Daniel Brisbin, Thomas Mayfield, Danny Embry, James White, Rylee Cunningham, Jed Stahl, Keegan Duncan, Michael McWilliams, Chase McLane, Stanley Hunt, Derek Parker, Matt Whyman, Tanner Phipps, James Givens, Luke Hardman, Hunter Gepner, Dylan Whitehead, Tristen Foster, Trey Mooney, Anthony Wilkerson, Bryce Mason, Sam Buzzard, Keegan Jones, Will Jeffries, J.D. Allen, Kendall Morrow, Angel Contreras, Kyler Overstreet, Aaron Moenning, Cooper Lucas, Isaiah Cleveland, Mike Jones, Stuart McKarus, Michael Danner, T.W. Ayers, Nick Gardner, Lane Fanning, Aaron Clements, Hayden Bartholomew, Seth Fullerton, Hunter Bayless, Andrew Hillman, Chase McKibben, Cameron Augusta, Lincoln Kaderly, Joseph Holden, Duncan Gepner, Trevor Medlin, Daniel Contreras, Cage Jordan, Dylan Hill, Isaac Collins, Landon Hardman, Chase Davey, Travis Bailey, Austin Dobbs, Brantly Duncan, Michael Henderson, Alex Burgess, B.J. Gammon, C.J. Maldanado, Caleb Gouge, Connor Duncan, Blake Felts and Wilson Miller. Head coach: Scott Bailey; assistant coaches: Thad Lundine, Brett Pettibon, Steven Bailey, Glen Cox, Iver Johnson, Eric England, Rick Piper, Dale Petton, Chris Wilkerson and Richard Grishow. *Lamar High School photo.*

Members of the 2016 Missouri Class 2A state champion Lamar Tigers included the following: Matt Whyman, Tanner Phipps. Luke Hardman, Hunter Gepner, Tristen Foster, Trey Mooney, Anthony Wilkerson, Bryce Mason, Sam Buzzard, Will Jeffries, J.D. Allen, Kendall Morrow, Angel Contreras, Kyler Overstreet, Aaron Moenning, Cooper Lucas, Isaiah Cleveland, Mike Jones, Eduardo Montayo, Stuart McKanus, Michael Danner, T.W. Ayers, Nick Gardner, Lane Fanning, Hunter Bayless, Andrew Hillman, Chase McKibben, Hayden Bartholomew, Cameron Augusta, Joseph Holder, Seth Fullerton, Duncan Gepner, Trevor Medlin, Daniel Contreras, Cage Jordan, Dylan Hill, Isaac Collins, Chase Davey, Travis Bailey, Brantly Duncan, Michael Henderson, Alex Burgess, B.J. Gammon, C.J. Maldanado, Caleb Gouge, Blake Felts, Wilson Miller, Dakota Bowman, J.D. Bishop, Payton Moenning, Branson Seaton, Stephen Davis, Donte Stahl, Trevon White, Wyatt Hull, Zachary Cano, Sam Mather, Tyler DeMoss, Ethan Seaton, Justin Walker, Carter Young, Zander Davis, Morgan Davis, Connor Brown, Carlos Paiz, Juan Juarez, George Weber, Ethan Krull, Connor O'Neal, Mark Costley, Saylor Sheat and Doran Hill. Head coach: Scott Bailey; assistant coaches: Brett Pettibon, Steven Bailey, Glen Cox, Colby Hall, Chris Wilkerson, Iver Johnson, Eric England, Rick Piper and Richard Grishow. *Lamar High School photo.*

Members of the 2017 Missouri Class 2A state champion Lamar Tigers included the following: Aaron Moenning, Cooper Lucas, Isaiah Cleveland, Mike Jones, Stuart McKarus, Michael Danner, T.W. Ayers, Colby Fiala, Nick Gardner, Lane Fanning, Seth Fullerton, Hunter Bayless, Andrew Hillman, Chase McKibben, Hayden Bartholomew, Cameron Augusta, Joseph Holder, B.J. Gammon, Trevor Medlin, Brett Mason, Daniel Contreras, Dylan Hill, Isaac Collins, Landon Hardman, Chase Davey, Travis Bailey, Brantly Duncan, Michael Henderson, Alex Burgess, C.J. Maldanado, Caleb Gouge, Blake Felts, Wilson Miller, J.D. Bishop, Branson Seaton, Stephen Davis, Donte Stahl, Wyatt Hull, Sam Mather, Tyler DeMoss, Ethan Seaton, Justin Walker, Carter Young, Morgan Davis, Connor Brown, Carlos Paiz, Juan Juarez, George Webber, Connor O'Neal, Mark Costley, Saylor Sheat, Cade Griffith, Case Tucker, Mason Guinn, Johnathan Contreras, Cody O'Sullivan, Ozzy Straw, Noah Osbourne, Sam O'Neal, Cadence Zupan, Draden Willhite, Ben Wilhelm, Phoeniz Pagacz, Rylan Wooldridge, Blane Shaw, Bailey Wright, Kaden McDowell, Mason Bartholomew and Carter Livingston. Head coach: Scott Bailey; assistant coaches: Brett Pettibon, Steven Bailey, Glen Cox, Jonathan Aldridge, Colby Hull, Chris Wilkerson, Iver Johnson, Eric England, Rick Piper and Richard Grishow. *Lamar High School photo.*

SOURCES

Chapter 1

Founding and naming of Lamar: Barton County Historical Society, *Barton County History and Families*, 10–11.

Quantrill's Raid, burning of Barton County Courthouse: Van Gilder, *Story of Barton County*, 11–12.

Nicholas Earp comes to Lamar, naming of Wyatt Earp: Tefertiller, *Wyatt Earp*.

Hogs running wild: "Lamar, Birthplace of President Harry S. Truman, Had Plenty Troubles in Early Days, Fame Is Widespread," *Sedalia Democrat*, September 25, 1949.

Earp's appointment praised: "Incorporated," *Southwest Missourian*, March 3, 1870.

Earp wedding, salary, drunken revelers, election: Van Gilder, *Story of Barton County*, 16; Barton County election records.

Death of Urilla Earp: Isenberg, *Wyatt Earp*, 59.

Urilla's burial site: Mike Surbrugg, "Tombstone II: First Wife of Lawman Wyatt Earp Gets New Grave Marker at Lamar," *Joplin Globe*, September 17, 1994.

Sale of house: Young, *Down Memory Lane*, 154–55.

Amanda Cobb description of Earp fight: Marvin L. Van Gilder, "The Present Is Linked Personally to the Past," *Lamar Press*, December 13, 1996.

Civil complaints: Wyatt Earp History Page, "Civil Complaints against Wyatt Earp."

Earp arrested, escapes: Van Gilder, *Story of Barton County*, 16.

Earp never spoke of Lamar: Barra, *Inventing Wyatt Earp*.

Johnathon Douglas Earp: Van Gilder, *Story of Barton County*, 16.

Everett Earp information: Helen Worden Erskine, "A Bit of Americana: The Earps Show Truman Birthplace," *Madison State Journal*, November 28, 1955.

Roy Earp: Virginia Coontz, "Oakland Officer, Kin of Famed Frontier Marshal May Get Title to House Where Truman Was Born," *Oakland Tribune*, August 31, 1947.

Truman telegram on death of Walter Earp: "Truman's Condolences on Lamar Man's Death," *Springfield Leader and Press*, December 24, 1945.

Information on Wyatt Earp photograph: Bulle, *Wyatt Earp (1869–1870)*.

Information on Wyatt Earp photograph, last paragraph: telephone interview with Marshall Bulle.

Chapter 2

Description of Truman property: Truman Birthplace Historic Site.

Description of businesses in Lamar: *Barton County Progress*, November 14, 1882.

Truman mule ad: *Lamar Democrat*, June 20, 1883.

Description of John Truman: Ferrell, *Harry S. Truman*.

Description of Lamar at time John Truman arrived: *Barton County Progress*, November 14, 1882.

Day Truman was born: "Lamar Was Busy the Day Truman Was Born," *Lamar Democrat*, May 3, 1984.

Dr. W.L. Griffin and Truman's birth: McCullough, *Truman*, 37.

Circuit Rider Washington Pease: Steinberg, *Man from Missouri*, 20.

Chapter 3

Lee Chiswell biographical information: "Death of Mr. Chiswell," *Frederick Citizen*, May 14, 1897.

Chiswell story: *Lamar Democrat*, May 8, 1884.

Chiswell modernizing Lamar newspaper: *Springfield News*, December 20, 1892.

Chiswell death: "Death of Mr. Chiswell," *Frederick Citizen*, May 14, 1897.

Arthur Aull early years: Stebbins, *All the News Is Fit to Print*, 2–6.

Luanna Aull quotes: *Lamar Democrat*, September 6, 1957.

Arthur Aull's rounds, local news coverage: Stebbins, *All the News Is Fit to Print*, 31.

Aull writing catches the eye of Ted Cook: Stebbins, *All the News Is Fit to Print*, 54–55.

Chapter 4

Birth, family of Jay Lynch: Barton County Historical Society, *Sad Legacy of Jay Lynch*, 3.

Arthur Aull description of Lynch murders: *Lamar Democrat*, March 6, 1919.

Lynch escape, accidental return to Lamar: Daetwyler, "Payoff at the End of a Rope."

Lynch captured: "Identification of Lynch Certain," *Joplin Globe*, May 17, 1919.

Frank O'Mara: "O'Mara Was Unwilling Double of Jay Lynch, Sent to Kansas Prison," *Joplin News Herald*, June 21, 1919.

Sheriff Sewell's quote: "Bad Man in Bates County Jail," *Butler Weekly Times and Bates County Record*, May 22, 1919.

Vernon County deputy quote, Lola Lynch description, Harlow planted elm tree, Lynch funeral: "Mob Hangs Slayer," *Kansas City Times*, May 29, 1919.

State legislature: Stebbins, *All the News Is Fit to Print*, 83.

Murder of Vernon County sheriff: "Vernon County Sheriff Slain," *Butler Weekly Times and Bates County Record*, July 18, 1919.

Moving of Jay Lynch's body: Barton County Historical Society, *Sad Legacy of Jay Lynch*.

Chapter 5

Letter to *Lamar Democrat*: *Lamar Democrat*, July 28, 1944.

Life Magazine article: "Harry Truman's Missouri," *Life*, June 25, 1945.

Walter Earp's death: "Dies in House Where Truman Was Born," *Joplin News Herald*, December 22, 1945.

Everett Earp sign: Harry S. Truman Library and Museum, "Man Pictured with a Sign, 'President Harry S. Truman Birth Place'."

Everett Earp charging for tours, trying to sell birthplace to state: "Lamar, Birthplace of President Harry S. Truman, Had Plenty of Trouble in Early Days; Fame Is Widespread," *Sedalia Democrat*, September 25, 1949.

Everett Earp's tall tales: Helen Worden Erskine, "A Bit of Americana: The Earps Show Truman Birthplace." *Madison State Journal*, November 28, 1955.

Everett Earp's death: "Everett M. Earp Dies in Old House of Harry Truman." *Joplin News Herald*, November 9, 1956.

UAW Purchase of Truman Birthplace: "Truman's Birthplace Bought for Shrine," *Neosho Daily News*, May 1, 1957.

Chapter 6

Chancellor achievements: Van Gilder, *Story of Barton County*, 19–20.

Restoring capital punishment in Missouri: Stebbins, *All the News Is Fit to Print*, 83.

Travelers Hotel history: Joe Davis, "The Travelers Hotel," *Lamar Democrat*, April 23, 2019.

Chancellor hands reins to Harold: Van Gilder, *Story of Barton County*, 20.

Idea for Barton County Memorial Hospital, bond issues pass: "Barton County Memorial Hospital Celebrates 65 Years," *Lamar Democrat*, August 20, 2014.

Chancellor named head of hospital committee: "H.C. Chancellor Heads Barton Hospital Group," *Joplin Globe*, March 23, 1946.

Second bond issue: "Barton County Memorial Hospital Celebrates 65 Years," *Lamar Democrat*, August 20, 2014.

Open house and dedication: "Plan Open House at Lamar Hospital," *Joplin Globe*, September 29, 1949.

H.C. Chancellor death: Missouri death certificate, Missouri Secretary of State.

Chapter 7

Chancellor dreamed of becoming a pilot: May 2019 author interview with Ione Chancellor.

College education: Barton County Historical Society, *Barton County History and Families*, 114.

Chancellor's early military career: Chancellor's unfinished memoirs, provided by Ione Chancellor.

Chancellor's heroism following first plane crash: Letter from Lieutenant Joe Young to Ione Chancellor, Chancellor family personal collection.

Chancellor receives medal: "Lamar Flier Given Medal for Bravery," *Joplin News Herald*, February 24, 1944.

Description of Chancellor's second crash landing: War Department letter to H.C. Chancellor.

German prison camp description: Mike Surbrugg, "Veterans of 4 Wars Recall Their Roles in Securing Peace," *Joplin Globe*, November 11, 1977.

Chancellor description of prison camp diet: "Richard Chancellor Tells Some of What Happened to Him in Germany," *Lamar Democrat*, June 5, 1945.

Bill Goade story: Surbrugg, "Veterans of 4 Wars."

Chancellor marriage, life after war: 2019 interview with Ione Chancellor.

Chapter 8

Description of robbery: "Lamar Sheriff and Son Slain," *Joplin News Herald*, August 17, 1944.

Description of discovery of sheriff and son: "Convict Seized in Slaying of Sheriff and Son," *Joplin Globe*, August 18, 1944.

Coroner's inquest interrupted: "Death of a Little Girl Broke Up Patterson Inquest," *Lamar Democrat*, August 22, 1944.

Results of coroner's inquest: "Coroner's Jury Reached Verdict Late Friday Afternoon," *Lamar Democrat*, August 25, 1944.

Bemis and Hastings in Skiatook: "Three Convicts to Be Quizzed in Lamar Slaying," *Joplin Globe*, August 19, 1944.

Patterson funeral: "Late Roy Patterson and His Son Sam Buried at Double Funeral," *Lamar Democrat*, August 22, 1944.

Hannah Oeltjen description: 2019 author interview with Hannah Oeltjen.

Arrest of Victor Monroe Rush, second accused killer: "Long Manhunt Preceded Apprehension of Two in Killing of Sheriff and Son," *Joplin News Herald*, August 28, 1945.

Rush confession: "Victor Monroe Rush Confesses to Killing of Sheriff Patterson and Son," *Lamar Democrat*, August 17, 1945.

Sentencing: "Life Terms to Killers of Sheriff and Son," *Neosho Daily Democrat*, October 23, 1945.

Huston brothers escape: "Two Lamar Slayers Returned to Prison," *Joplin Globe*, November 23, 1948.

Chapter 9

Letter from Harry Truman to Bess from Connor Hotel: Ferrell, ed., *Dear Bess*, 315–17.

Truman first campaign visit to Lamar in 1934: "Judge Truman Candidate for U.S. Senate Stops Off Briefly in Lamar Which Is His Birthplace," *Lamar Democrat*, May 25, 1934.

Second Truman visit to Lamar in 1934 campaign: "Judge Truman Jackson County Candidate for U.S. Senate before He Went to the World War Engaged in Farming," *Lamar Democrat*, July 31, 1934.

Arthur Aull backs Lloyd Stark: "Whom Does Pendergast Hate the Most and Why" and "This Is the Man Who Overthrew the Pendergast Machine," *Lamar Democrat*, July 10, 1940.

Aull backing Stark, discouraging votes for Milligan: "Honorable Maurice Milligan Speaks from Lamar Bandstand," *Lamar Democrat*, July 30, 1940.

Chapter 10

Decision to invite Truman to Lamar: "Harry Truman Invited to Make His First Campaign Address in Lamar," *Lamar Democrat*, July 25, 1944.

Truman's letter to Bess: Ferrell, ed., *Dear Bess*, 508–10.

Hannegan announcement: "Truman Probably Will Open Campaign in Lamar," *Joplin Globe*, August 9, 1944.

Planning meeting in Lamar: "Make the Plans for the Truman Meeting," *Lamar Democrat*, August 18, 1944.

Fears that Joplin would steal the event, River conversation with Boyle: "We Believe Mr. Boyle Now Knows That the Meeting Is to Be at Lamar," *Lamar Democrat*, August 29, 1944.

Truman arrival in Joplin: "Truman Arrives, Confident Ticket Will Work in Missouri," *Joplin News Herald*, August 30, 1944.

Truman visit to Camp Crowder: "City Entertains Truman on Eve of Notification," *Joplin Globe*, August 31, 1944.

Camp Crowder history: Amick, *Camp Crowder*, 1, 15, 77.

Lamar weather, Truman Day description: "Lamar Puts up Bunting in the Rain," *Joplin Globe*, August 31, 1944.

Welcoming of press, dignitaries: *Lamar Democrat*, September 1, 1944.

Margaret Truman's views of Lamar: Truman, *Harry S. Truman*, 186.

Pickpockets: "Pickpockets in Lamar on Truman Day," *Lamar Democrat*, September 4, 1944.

Truman arrival in Lamar: "Lamar Impressed by Glamor of Big Political Show," *Joplin News Herald*, September 1, 1944.

How Truman speech, national coverage came about: "J. Leonard Reinsch Oral History Interview," Harry S. Truman Library and Museum.

Death of Donald Quillin, "Donald Quillin Killed in Action," *Lamar Democrat*, August 12, 1944.

Dress of those attending Truman Day: Video, Truman Birthplace, Lamar, Missouri.

Program for Truman Day: "City Entertains Truman on Eve of Notification."

John McClellan official opening of campaign: "Lamar Impressed by Glamor of Big Political Show," *Joplin News Herald*, September 1, 1944.

Truman speech: "Text of Truman's Speech Accepting His Nomination for Vice President," *New York Times*, September 1, 1944.

Martha Truman reaction: "Lamar Impressed by Glamor of Big Political Show."

Chapter 11

Profile of Arthur Aull: "Aull Prints All the News," *Life*, February 26, 1945.

Hearst columnist Ted Cook: Stebbins, *All the News Is Fit to Print*.

Next several paragraphs: "Aull Prints All the News."

Second Life Magazine article: "Harry Truman's Missouri," *Life*, June 26, 1945.

Madeleine attended University of Missouri: "Lamar Newspaper a Family Affair." *Springfield Leader and Press*, November 12, 1972.

Madeleine quote on attending MU: "Lamar Newspaper a Family Affair."

Attack on Arthur Aull: "Editor Is Beaten by an Irate Woman," *Joplin Globe*, August 12, 1943.

Death of Arthur Aull: "Arthur Aull Is Dead," *Lamar Democrat*, May 11, 1948.

Condolences from Harry S. Truman: Stebbins, *All the News Is Fit to Print*, 1.

Prejudices faced by Madeleine: 2019 author interview with Dorothy Parks.

Stanley White named business manager: "Stanley White Becomes Lamar Democrat Business Manager," *Lamar Democrat*, September 29, 1953.

Democrat's financial picture improves: Stebbins, *All the News Is Fit to Print*, 136.

Democrat buys *Lamar Journal*: "Missouri Notes," *Kansas City Times*, September 13, 1954.

Madeleine's views on civil rights: "Two Wrongs Don't Make a Right," *Le Mars Daily Sentinel*, June 25, 1963.

Madeleine's views on women's liberation: "Funeral Slated for Ex-Editor," *Springfield Leader and Press*, November 22, 1977.

Democrat sells to Kirkpatrick family: "Historic Lamar Newspaper Is Purchased," *Carthage Press*, November 1, 1972.

Reasons for selling *Democrat*: Stebbins, *All the News Is Fit to Print*, 137.

Never returned to *Democrat*: 2019 author interview with Dorothy Parks.

Madeleine interview with *St. Louis Post-Dispatch*: "Editor Madeleine's Last Damn," *St. Louis Post-Dispatch*, November 1, 1972.

Father's advice, Madeleine's death: "Funeral Slated for Ex-Editor."

Chapter 12

Mules to be in inaugural parade: "Mules Assured Spot in Inaugural Parade," *Joplin Globe*, January 8, 1949.

Brother Adams quote to United Press: "Lamar, Mo Sending Blue Ribbon Mules to Inaugural March," *Keokuk Daily Gate*, January 4, 1949.

Description of mules: "Mules from President Truman's Birthplace to Inauguration," *Joplin Globe*, January 13, 1949.

Billee Bob Adams background: Barton County Historical Society, *Barton County History and Families*, 102.

He knows a lot about mules quote: "Lamar, Mo Sending Blue Ribbon Mules to Inaugural March."

Details on Kansas City mule show: "Harry Truman Enjoys Role at Missouri Mule Exhibit," *Moberly Monitor-Index*, October 16, 1963.

Chapter 13

Truman call to Loyd Gathman: Randy Turner, "Gathman Remembers," *Lamar Democrat*, May 3, 1984.

Plans for Barton County Historical Society: Marvin L. Van Gilder, "President Truman Adds His Blessing to Plan for Barton County Historical Society," *Lamar Daily Journal*, August 9, 1954.

Gathman recollections of Truman visit: Turner, "Gathman Remembers."

City workers prepare for Truman visit: "To Dress Up Old Town," *Lamar Democrat*, April 2, 1959.

Reporters arrive, weather conditions: "A Great Day in Lamar," *Lamar Democrat*, April 23, 1959.

Background on re-creation of Oregon Trail, Gordon Serpa, "Trek by Wagon Train Starts April 11, Missouri to Oregon," *Myrtle Point Herald*, February 26, 1959.

Truman westward ho: "Mule Train Heads West," *Paducah Sun*, April 21, 1959.

Truman Arrives in Lamar: Harry S. Truman Library and Museum, "Truman Arrives for Dedication of Birthplace in Lamar."

"A little different than I remember it": James C. Millstone, "Glad to Be Dug Up While Still Alive," *St. Louis Post-Dispatch*, April 20, 1959.

Truman schedule, description of activities, quotes from officials, Symington address: "Throngs Converge in Lamar as Ex-President Truman's Birthplace Given Missouri," *Carthage Evening Press*, April 20, 1959.

Donald Braker quotes: Millstone, "Glad to Be Dug Up While Still Alive."

Truman signing register: Register at Truman Birthplace.

Chapter 14

Gerald Gilkey on the Lamar Square, first automobile, courtship of Gerald, Betty Gilkey, early marriage, Betty Gilkey's wartime job, Gilkey returns from Aleutians, calls at home, Gilkey never tempted to quit: 2019 author interview with Betty Gilkey.

Gilkey jobs after graduation: John Gilkey, "Happy Birthday, Mr. Mayor," *Lamar Press*, April 18, 1997.

Wedding secret revealed: "Sheldon Couple Weds," *Joplin Globe*, June 20, 1942.

Gilkey passing time in the Aleutians, Gilkey returning from Aleutians, Stan White talks Gilkey into running for city council, Norbert Heim asks Gilkey to run for mayor, mayoral job had no effect on business, calls at home, Gilkey's last council meeting: 2019 author interview with Steve Gilkey.

Second paragraph, coming home from Aleutians: 2019 author interview with Steve Gilkey.

Gilkey success selling cars, offer from Loyd Gathman: Gilkey, "Happy Birthday, Mr. Mayor."

Angry constituents coming into car dealership: 2019 author interview with Courtney Gardner.

Free electricity, *Paul Harvey Show*, Gilkey successes as mayor: Turner, "Remembering Gerald Gilkey."

Unveiling of Gilkey portrait: Turner, "The City Was His Love."

Chapter 15

Lamar's prominence in the U.S. Navy and Coast Guard: "Lamar All Out for U.S. Navy," *Joplin Globe,* June 17, 1943.

Memories of Lamar living in duplex, working for Ottawa newspaper, always wanted to write: "Mid-West Pastor's Daughter Is Commander of the SPARS," *Kansas City Star,* February 7, 1943.

Stratton's father was Baptist Church minister in Lamar: church directories, Barton County Historical Society.

"Were You Ever a Bad Little Girl?": "Newly Appointed Director of SPARS Has Wide Background in Organizing," *Joplin Globe,* December 1, 1942.

First full-time dean of women at Purdue, Legion of Merit, International Monetary Fund, Girl Scouts: Purdue University, "Dorothy C. Stratton, Purdue's First Dean of Women, Dies at 107."

Dorothy Stratton joins navy, colleague says you can't do that, Stratton modest about her title and rank: Obama White House Archives, "Remarks by the First Lady at Christening of U.S. Coast Guard Cutter Stratton in Pascagoula, Mississippi."

Time between joining navy and formation of SPARS: "Newly Appointed Director of SPARS Has Wide Background in Organizing."

Chapter 16

Ensign Shapley's speech, Daubin time at Annapolis, *Lucky Bag*: Richard L. Stokes, "Lamar, Mo. Home Town of the U.S. Navy Submarine Chiefs in Atlantic and Pacific, Also Other Officers and SPARS Director," *St. Louis Post-Dispatch,* June 13, 1943.

March 31, 1943 speech in New London, Connecticut: "A Submarine Man Must Be Tough," *Pottstown Mercury,* April 4, 1943.

Navy Distinguished Service Medal: Military Times, Hall of Valor Project, "Freeland Allyn Daubin."

Daubin's death: "RAdm Daubin Services Today," *Coronado Eagle and Journal,* October 29, 1959.

Chapter 17

Daubin encourages Lockwood to apply for U.S. Naval Academy: Richard L. Stokes, "Lamar, Mo. Hometown of the U.S. Navy Submarine Chiefs in Atlantic and Pacific, Also Other Officers and SPARS Director," *St. Louis Post-Dispatch*, June 13, 1943.

Lockwood service record: Military Museum, "Californians in the Military: Vice Admiral Charles A Lockwood, Jr."

Lockwood improvements in weaponry: "Director of Effective U.S. Submarine War in Pacific Visits Friends Here," *Syracuse Post-Standard*, March 14, 1955.

Fresh vegetables and ice cream: Australian National Submarine Museum, "Vice Admiral Charles A. Lockwood USN."

Differences between Lockwood, Ralph Waldo Christie: Blair, *Silent Victory*, 414.

Statistics on how submarine did under Lockwood's command: "Director of Effective U.S. Submarine War in Pacific Visits Friends Here," *Syracuse Post-Standard*, March 14, 1955.

Lockwood and the Nautilus: Weapons and Warfare, "Cold War Submarine Warfare I."

Books by Charles Lockwood: Amazon.com, "Charles Lockwood author page."

Lockwood movies: Internet Movie Database, "Charles A. Lockwood."

Ronald Reagan and Nancy Davis only film together: Rebecca Keegan, "Nancy and Ronald Reagan's Sole Film Together, 'Hellcats of the Navy,' Previewed Decades of Devotion," *Los Angeles Times*, March 7, 2016.

Death of Charles Lockwood: "Leader of U.S. Sub Fleet in War Dies," *Kansas City Star*, June 7, 1967.

Chapter 18

Associated Press article on three admirals: Richard L. Stokes, "Lamar, Mo. Home Town of the U.S. Navy Submarine Chiefs in Atlantic and Pacific, Also Other Officers and SPARS Director," *St. Louis Post-Dispatch*, June 13, 1943.

Combs family background: Barton County Historical Society, *Barton County History and Families*, 118.

Distinguished Service Medals: Military Times, Hall of Valor Project, "Thomas Selby Combs." Five commands: "Vice Admiral Retiring," *New York Times*, March 30, 1960.

Naval commands, death: "Admiral Combs, 44 Years in Navy," *New York Times*, December 11, 1964.

Chapter 19

Hutchens Manufacturing, J.G. Doyle, Lawn-Boy in Lamar: Barton County Historical Society records.

Announcement of closing of Lawn-Boy plant: "Lawn Boy to Move," *Joplin Globe*, July 9, 1963.

Birth of Tom O'Sullivan, first business, "Lamar Industrial Titan Dies," *Joplin Globe*, March 13, 2004.

Tom O'Sullivan well organized, pleasure in helping the little guy, generosity: Email to author from Betty Thieman

Idea for TV stands, opening plant in Japan: Kratz, *Simply the Best*, 19–22.

Dispute with Koelling: "Sullivan Industries Leaving Japan, Missouri," *Sullivan Tri-County News*, December 6, 1956.

Threat of labor vote closing O'Sullivan Industries: "OIC Concerned over Possible Loss of Local Industry," *Owensville Gasconade County Republican*, January 28, 1960.

Advertisement after union vote: Classified ad, *Owensville Gasconade County Republican*, February 11, 1960.

Dan O'Sullivan sales skills: Kratz, *Simply the Best*, 31.

Gerald Medlin, move to Lamar: Kratz, *Simply the Best*, 27.

Lamar workers perfect fit: Charlene Pearcy, "Lamar Given Shot in Arm with News of Firm Moving into Lawn Boy Plant," *Joplin Globe*, September 4, 1964.

Company history 1990–2005: Company Histories, "O'Sullivan Industries Holdings, Inc."

Creation of O'Sullivan Properties: Kratz, *Simply the Best*, 48.

Peggy Hillman, Lamar High School bond issue: Randy Turner, "Lamar High School: Peggy Hillman's Dream Lives On," *Lamar Press*, September 5, 1996.

Football Stadium named after O'Sullivan: Turner, *Sports Talk Memories*, 59.

Bankruptcy: Georgia Northern Bankruptcy Court filings.

Chapter 20

Background of Evan R. Daniels: Turner, "Questions Raised about Lamar's Newest Industry."

Daniels hired lobbyist: Missouri Ethics Commission records, Missouri Ethics Commission.

Henry and Esther Bailey: Judy Probert, "Bailey Era Coming to an End at Lamar High," *Lamar Democrat*, February 23, 1989.

Scott Bailey biographical information: 2021 author interview.

Jared Beshore quotes about 2011, 2020 championships: 2021 author interview.

State Championship games, scores: Missouri State High School Activities Association.

Hiring of Jared Beshore: Amanda Sullivan, "Former MSU Captain, Lamar High Star Jared Beshore Named Tigers' Head Football Coach," *Springfield News-Leader*, March 30, 2020.

Team rosters: Lamar High School.

BIBLIOGRAPHY

Books

Amick, Jeremy. *Camp Crowder: A History*. Charleston, SC: Arcadia Publishing, 2019.

Barra, Allen. *Inventing Wyatt Earp: His Life and Many Legends*. Lincoln: University of Nebraska Press, 2009.

Barton County Historical Society. *Barton County History and Families*. Sikeston, MO: Acclaim Press, 2015.

————. *Sad Legacy of Jay Lynch*. Lamar, MO: Barton County Historical Society, n.d.

Blair, Clay. *Silent Victory: U.S. Submarine War against Japan*. Annapolis, MD: Naval Institute Press, 2001.

Bulle, Marshall. *Wyatt Earp (1869–1870): The Lost Story*. N.p.: self-published, 2020.

Ferrell, Robert H. *Harry S. Truman: A Life*. Columbia: University of Missouri Press, 2013.

————, ed. *Dear Bess: The Letters from Harry to Bess Truman*. New York: W.W. Norton and Company, 1983.

Isenberg, Andrew C. *Wyatt Earp: A Vigilante Life*. New York: Farrar, Straus and Giroux, 2013.

Kratz, Jennifer. *Simply the Best: The O'Sullivan Story*. Lamar, MO: O'Sullivan Industries, 2000.

McCullough, David. *Truman*. New York: Simon and Schuster, 1992.

Stebbins, Chad. *All the News Is Fit to Print: Profile of a Country Editor*. Columbia: University of Missouri Press, 1998.

Steinberg, Alfred. *The Man from Missouri: The Life and Times of Harry S. Truman*. New York: Putnam, 1962.

Tefertiller, Casey. *Wyatt Earp: The Life behind the Legend*. New York: Wiley, 1999.

Truman, Margaret. *Harry S. Truman*. New York: William Morrow, 1973.

Turner, Randy. *Sports Talk Memories*. N.p.: self-published, 2015.

Van Gilder, Marvin L. *The Story of Barton County*. N.p.: self-published, 1972.

Young, Reba. *Down Memory Lane*. N.p.: self-published, 1994. Republished as *Truman's Birthplace Lamar Missouri*. New Orleans: Pelican Publishing, 2004.

Magazine Articles

Cauley, John R. "Aull Prints All the News." *Life*, February 26, 1945.
Daetwyler, Wallace. "Payoff at the End of a Rope." *True Detective*, December 1942.
Eisenstadt, Alfred (photographer). "Harry Truman's Missouri." *Life*, June 26, 1945.

Newspapers

Barton County (MO) Progress
*Butler (MO) Weekly Times and
    Bates County Record*
Carthage (MO) Press
Coronado (CO) Eagle and Journal
Frederick (MD) Citizen
Joplin (MO) Globe
Joplin (MO) News Herald
Kansas City (MO) Star
Kansas City (MO) Times
Keokuk (IA) Daily Gate
Lamar (MO) Daily Journal
Lamar (MO) Democrat
Lamar (MO) Press
Lamar (MO) Southwest Missourian
Le Mars (IA) Daily Sentinel
Los Angeles (CA) Times
Madison (WI) State Journal

Moberly (MO) Monitor-Index
Myrtle Point (OR) Herald
Neosho (MO) Daily Democrat
Neosho (MO) Daily News
New York (NY) Times
Oakland (CA) Tribune
*Owensville (MO) Gasconade County
    Republican*
Paducah (KY) Sun
Pottstown (PA) Mercury
Sedalia (MO) Democrat
Springfield (MO) Leader and Press
Springfield (MO) News
Springfield (MO) News-Leader
St. Louis (MO) Post-Dispatch
Sullivan (MO) Tri-County News
Syracuse (NY) Post-Standard

Websites

Amazon. "Charles Lockwood author page." www.amazon.com.
Australian National Submarine Museum. "Vice Admiral Charles A. Lockwood USN." https://ansmpilot.org.au.
Company Histories. "O'Sullivan Industries Holdings Inc." www.company-histories.com.
Internet Movie Database. "Charles A. Lockwood." https://imdb.com.
Harry S. Truman Library and Museum. "J. Leonard Reinsch Oral History Interview." www.trumanlibrary.gov.
———. "Man Pictured with a Sign, 'President Harry S. Truman Birth Place.'" www.trumanlibrary.gov.
———. "Truman Arrives for Dedication of Birthplace in Lamar." www.trumanlibrary.gov.

Military Museum. "Californians in the Military: Vice Admiral Charles A Lockwood, Jr." www.militarymuseum.org.

Military Times. Hall of Valor Project. "Charles Lockwood, Navy Distinguished Service Medal." https://valor.militarytimes.com.

———. "Thomas Selby Combs—Navy Distinguished Service Medal." https://valor.militarytimes.com.

Missouri Ethics Commission. "Lobbyist Searches." www.mec.mo.gov.

Missouri Secretary of State. "Henry C. Chancellor Death Certificate." www.sos.mo.gov.

Missouri State High School Activities Association. MSHSAA State Championships. "Football State Championships." www.mshsaa.org.

Obama White House Archives. "Remarks by the First Lady at Christening of U.S. Coast Guard Cutter Stratton in Pascagoula, Mississippi." https:obamawhitehouse.archives.gov.

The Turner Report. "The City Was His Love." July 17, 2006. http://rturner229.blogspot.com.

———. "Questions Raised about Lamar's Newest Industry." November 4, 2007. https://rturner229.blogspot.com.

———. "Remembering Gerald Gilkey." September 29, 2005. https://rturner229.blogspot.com.

University of Purdue. "Dorothy C. Stratton, Purdue's First Full-Time Dean of Women, Dies at 107." www.purdue.edu.

Weapons and Warfare. "Cold War Submarine Warfare I." https://weaponsandwarfare.com.

Wyatt Earp History Page. "Civil Complaints against Wyatt Earp." wyattearp.net.

INDEX

ABOUT THE AUTHOR

Randy Turner is a retired middle school English teacher who worked twenty-two years as a newspaper reporter and editor in southwest Missouri, primarily at the *Lamar Democrat* and *Carthage Press*, earning more than fifty awards for investigative reporting, spot news reporting and feature writing. He is the author of thirteen nonfiction books, including *5:41: Stories from the Joplin Tornado* and *The Buck Starts Here: Harry S. Truman and the City of Lamar*, as well as three novels.